Frank O'Connor

THE IRISH WRITERS SERIES
James F. Carens, General Editor

FRANK O'CONNOR

James H. Matthews

Lewisburg
BUCKNELL UNIVERSITY PRESS
London: ASSOCIATED UNIVERSITY PRESSES

© 1976 by Associated University Presses, Inc.

Associated University Presses, Inc.
Cranbury, New Jersey 08512

Associated University Presses
108 New Bond Street
London W1Y OQX, England

Library of Congress Cataloging in Publication Data

Matthews, James H.   1942-
  Frank O'Connor.

  (The Irish writers series)
  Bibliography: p.
  1. O'Donovan, Michael, 1903–1966—Criticism and
interpretation.
PR6029.D58Z75   828   75-125470
ISBN 0-8387-7756-2
ISBN-0-8387-7609-4 pbk.

Contents

Preface

Few readers familiar with the literature of Ireland in the twentieth century would be unaware of the name of Frank O'Connor. Yet, though blessed with liberal acclaim, O'Connor's writing has received only selective regard. In line with the aims of this Irish Writers Series, my task is to present for general consideration the writings of Frank O'Connor, hoping to isolate a few of his main concerns and methods. By way of limitation, I will offer no specific treatment of: 1) O'Connor's plays, because they are still unpublished and because all but two were written in collaboration with Hugh Hunt; 2) his own poetry, except in passing, because it represents little that cannot be seen in the other writing; and 3) the many essays, reviews, and broadcasts, because most of them appear in varied form in his books. I especially regret that my limited acquaintance with the Irish language forbids the kind of examination of his translations that they deserve.

Acknowledgments

I wish to thank Mrs. Harriet O'Donovan Sheehy and Mrs. Evelyn Garbery for their gracious help and encouragement. Brendan Kennelly, Maurice Sheehy, and Thomas Kilroy all helped at various stages of my study and deserve particular thanks. I am grateful also to the University of Tulsa, the Oklahoma Consortium for Higher Education, and Eckerd College for providing financial support for travel and research.

Grateful acknowledgment is extended to Alfred A. Knopf, Inc., for permission to quote from the following copyrighted works of Frank O'Connor: AN ONLY CHILD, MY FATHER'S SON, DOMESTIC RELATIONS, and A SET OF VARIATIONS.

Citations from British editions of Frank O'Connor's work reprinted by permission of A. D. Peters and Company.

And special thanks to Pat Bouwman for careful reading and to my wife, Sheila, for caring.

Chronology

1903   Born on 17 September in Cork, Michael Francis O'Donovan.

1914   At St. Patrick's National School comes under tutelage of Corkery.

1918   Joins First Brigade of the Irish Republican Army.

1923   In detention at Gormanstown Internment Camp.

1924–   Teaches Irish in rural schools; librarian in
1928   Sligo, Wicklow, and Cork. Poems and essays appearing in *The Irish Statesman.*

1928   To Dublin as librarian in Pembroke.

1931   First volume of stories, *Guests of the Nation.*

1932   First novel, *The Saint and Mary Kate,* and first translations of Irish poetry, *Wild Bird's Nest* (Cuala).

1935   Appointed to Board of Directors of the Abbey Theatre.

1936   *Three Old Brothers. Bones of Contention.*

1937   First broadcast on Radio Eireann. Made Managing Director of the Abbey. With Hugh Hunt produces "In the Train" and "The Invincibles." *The Big Fellow.*

1938   *Lords and Commons* (Cuala). "Moses' Rock" (in collaboration with Hugh Hunt) and "Time's Pocket" produced at the Abbey. Resigns post in

Pembroke Library. Marries Evelyn Bowen
Speaight.

1939 *Fountain of Magic* (Cuala). Forced to resign
from the Board of Directors of the Abbey
Theatre after the death of Yeats.

1940 *Dutch Interior* (officially banned on 10 July).
Lament for Art O'Leary (Cuala).

1941 *The Statue's Daughter* produced at the Gate
Theatre. Working with the BBC in London.

1942 *Three Tales* (Cuala).

1944 *Crab Apple Jelly.*

1946 *Selected Stories. The Midnight Court* (banned
on 30 April).

1947 *Irish Miles. Art of the Theatre. The Common
Chord* (banned on 12 December).

1948 *Road to Stratford.* Separated from his wife.

1950 *Leinster, Munster, and Connaught.*

1951 *Traveller's Samples* (banned on 20 April). Teaches
at Northwestern University and Harvard.

1952 Divorce. Death of his mother on 10 November.

1953 *The Stories of Frank O'Connor.* Marries Harriet
Rich.

1954 *More Stories.*

1956 *Mirror in the Roadway.*

1956 *Domestic Relations.*

1959 *Book of Ireland. Kings, Lords, & Commons.*

1961 *An Only Child.* While teaching at Stanford
University suffers a stroke. Returns to Ireland.

1962 Awarded D. Litt. from Trinity College, Dublin.

1963 *Little Monasteries.*

1964 *The Lonely Voice. Collection Two.*

1966 Death on 10 March in Dublin: burial 12 March,
Dean's Grange.

Frank O'Connor

1

Improvising an Irish Writer

Writers in general, and Irish writers in particular, are customarily cast as persons of massive contradiction and cultural alienation. In the case of Michael O'Donovan/Frank O'Connor that role is neither hard to assign nor easy to assess. By his outspoken response to the public affairs of Ireland, O'Connor antagonized partisans of every persuasion. A dedicated rebel, he nevertheless attacked the pettiness and irrelevancies of post-Revolution Ireland. Though imprisoned during the Civil War, he was later to write a fiercely sympathetic biography of Michael Collins. And despite his reputation as a notorious anti-cleric, he wrote some of his most gentle stories about priests. With all the arrogance and eccentricity of the self-taught, Frank O'Connor learned by doing and fought his way through one contradiction after another.

Like most Irish writers of his generation—that of Sean O'Faolain, Patrick Kavanagh, and Austin Clarke—O'Connor was caught between the fading generation of the Literary Revival and the Revolution and the rising force of the post-World War II generation. The trick for his generation was to synthesize the values, while rejecting the dangers, of nationalism on the one hand and internationalism on the other. National pride, while stimulating great inner energies and fostering a firm sense of identity, also served to restrict the vision of the Irish people, thereby creating a self-defeating parochialism. By contrast, the new international outlook in art, commerce, and politics offered a fresh climate of expansiveness and tolerance; its unhealthy side effects, at least for Ireland and Irish writers, were anonymity and impermanence. Frank O'Connor and the others were trapped between contradictory allegiances. Always between, they appeared to be middle-aged, middle-class, middle-everything. In the 1920s O'Connor was a veteran of the rebellion and an inheritor of the Literary Movement. In the 1930s he was an established writer, to be rejected by the young "exiles" in Europe. In the forties and fifties he was starting all over again.

The facts of O'Connor's life are at once simple and obscure. He was born on September 17, 1903, in Cork and lived in slum tenements on Blarney Lane and Summerhill in that curiously provincial city. By the age of fourteen he had left school, but not before he had come under the tutelage of the writer and critic Daniel Corkery. He fought with the I. R. A. in the Revolution and stood with the Republicans in the ensuing Civil War. After his release from Gormanstown Internment Camp he taught Irish in rural schools, directed a theatre group in Cork, and served as a librarian in Sligo, Cork, and Wicklow. During the 1930s he administered the Pembroke Library in Dublin, managed the Abbey Theatre for three years, and found time to write two novels, two volumes of stories, one volume of poetry, three volumes of translations, three plays, and a biography. By 1939 O'Connor had licked his wounds from the bitter Abbey feud, mourned the death of Yeats, married a young actress named Evelyn Bowen Speaight, and resigned his post as librarian. From then on he was strictly a writer.

From *An Only Child* and *My Father's Son* one might easily suppose that nothing much happened to Frank O'Connor after the death of Yeats, when, in fact, his life became much more complicated and turbulent. By any reckoning 1940 marks a dividing line for all Irish writers. Yeats was dead and Joyce soon would be. A new international war had broken out, testing Irish neutrality. By then Ireland had settled into post-Revolutionary incrustation and mediocrity. Censorship of books and newspapers had brought an intellectual darkness, forcing many young writers to follow Joyce into exile. Others like O'Connor and O'Faolain chose what Kiely calls "spiritual exile." Actually, there was nowhere else to go.

By 1950 O'Connor was more or less cut off from everyone in Ireland. At his wife's insistence he had gone to London in 1941 to work for the Ministry of Information and for the BBC. A complex set of circumstances after the war led to his separation from Evelyn and to their eventual divorce. Moreover, he was all but officially blacklisted from employment in Dublin. Hector Legge, editor of the *Sunday Independent*, ran O'Connor's "Ben Mayo" series under total secrecy; the pseudonym "Frank O'Connor" had become to the Irish "common reader" linked with sexuality and impiety. Eventually, writing and broadcasting became insufficient to meet O'Connor's financial responsibilities; his family had increased and he had

somehow amassed a considerable tax debt. Therefore,
by 1950 Frank O'Connor had created for himself a
vacuum in Ireland.

In 1951, unable to support himself in Dublin, and
with divorce proceedings inching through British courts,
O'Connor left to teach in the United States. Actually
his exile, if indeed his American sojourn can be called
that, was more of a personal than a professional neces-
sity. Gradually, he began to receive acclaim, especially
from readers in America and on the Continent. His
stories and autobiographical pieces drew exuberant
attention as they appeared in *The New Yorker*. It
wasn't long before his "exile" ended and he returned
with his young wife, Harriet, to Ireland. His return
corresponded with the sense of renewal evident in all
of his later writing. Through it all, O'Connor had held
tenaciously to his writing, so that despite the barrenness
of exile and the bitterness of separation he managed
to maintain his artistic integrity and personal identity.
James Plunkett in *The Gems She Wore* describes O'Connor as having toward the end of his life "the air of
someone who had found where he belonged, not an
easy thing for a writer to achieve in the Ireland of his
time." Actually, during the last decade of his life
O'Connor wrote more than in any period of his life.
What he wrote was neither whim of dotage nor a new
departure. It was, rather, the culmination of a life
of contradictory devotions and struggles.

Despite the strong personal element in most of his
writing, O'Connor was actually reserved about himself,
particularly about the facts of his private life. Thomas
Flanagan is more than correct when he calls *An Only
Child* "a book of concealed reticences." The same can
be said of the second autobiographical volume, *My*

Father's Son. Together these two books, written in
the last decade of O'Connor's life, represent the backward glance of the aging and successful writer. Having
improvised his way to a secure and indelible form,
O'Connor began drawing more and more on his own
experiences.

An Only Child is a cautious story, revealing those
attachments which gave rise to the sympathetic side of
his writing. The indignant scourge of Irish manners is
kept nicely in check by the celebrant of the "little guy."
Primarily, the book consists of sharp, highly dramatic
vignettes of his family, his friends, and his neighbors.
The significance these simple and unknown people had
for him indicates the kind of man and the kind of
writer Frank O'Connor was.

It's not really until the third section of *An Only Child*
that O'Connor speaks of himself. But underneath the
entire book is an awareness that the little boy became a
writer. O'Connor doesn't seem to see anything favorable
or unfavorable about anything in his life; his credentials
as an Irishman, as an artist, or as a rebel have little to do
with pedigree. That he became a writer against great
odds was simply the way things worked out. "I came to
literature as I fancy a great many people come to it,
because they need companionship, and a wider and
more civilized form of life than they can find in the
world about them." He educated himself for the same
reasons that he read novels and boys' weeklies—to
escape the loneliness of being an only child and of
being poor. However, O'Connor's tone disallows pity
because his youthful improvisations all seem more
laughable than pathetic, more full of wide-eyed en-
thusiasm than depression.

Given his natural inclination to dreaming and other

impractical enterprises, O'Connor's early devotion to
Daniel Corkery is easy to understand. Corkery was a
passionate nationalist; he was also a painter, a writer,
a lover of music. O'Connor left school at fourteen but
continued to learn Irish and to believe in Corkery's holy
cause. With the same naive fervor with which he plunged
into languages, he also took to revolution. For Michael
O'Donovan, "smart boy" of Harrington Square, it was

> a safety valve for my own angry emotions. Indeed, it
> would be truer to say that the Irish nation and myself
> were both engaged in an elaborate process of improvisa-
> tion. I was improvising an education I could not afford,
> and the country was improvising a revolution it could
> not afford.

Like his mother perhaps, O'Connor believed that he
could make the world more palatable. That he always
tried is testimony to his romanticism; that he knew in
the end that the reach exceeds the grasp is the mark
of his realism.

The Revolution and Civil War served to crystallize
some of the contradictions in O'Connor's life. Between
the nostalgic idealism of Daniel Corkery and the violent reality of battle, O'Connor found that point of
uneasy truth where one must always reject a little and
accept a little from both sides. Thus, the final episode
of *An Only Child* is carefully elaborated to indicate that
rebellion was more than an interlude, more than a
pause in a young idealist's plunge toward realism. It
was a sort of graduation, a decisive departure. In the
internment camp he opposed, against great pressure,
the hunger strike organized by the most fanatic Republicans. "It was clear to me that we were all going

mad, and yet I could see no way out. The imagination
seems to paralyze not only the critical faculty but the
ability to act upon the most ordinary instinct of self-
preservation." The adventure of the political revolution, elaborated so clearly in his early stories, was
replaced by the difficult and often unpopular position
of personal revolution. When the imagination of the
community begins to dominate the imagination of the
artist, he must back away. When O'Connor saw the
hungry prisoners feeding hysterically like so many pigs,
he "knew it was the end of our magical improvisation."
On that sad note the book ends. But the loss was not
altogether without gain: the loss of illusion was accompanied by a new freedom and the loss of religion
by new faith. So Michael/Frank turned "finally from
poetry to story-telling, to the celebration of those who
for me represented all I should ever know of God."

My Father's Son begins where *An Only Child* left
off—in a vacuum of loss and disaffection. In the second
volume he continues his defense of literature and the
creative improvising of life. That defense rings especially
earnest, for instance, in his portrait of Father Tim
Traynor, a man ill-suited by his passionate temperament
for the priesthood. "All the imaginative improvisation
was only the outward expression of a terrible inward
loneliness, loneliness that was accentuated by his calling." O'Connor did not make a habit of comparing the
artist to the priest. But just as he was acutely aware of
the loneliness of the only child, so he always seemed to
be aware that in Ireland priests and artists are lonely
outcasts, "cut off from ordinary intercourse in a way
that seems unknown in other countries."

Having lavished such fond attention on his mother in

An Only Child, he acknowledges in *My Father's Son* a harsher, more contentious heritage. To his mother O'Connor attributes his habit of dreaming. From his father he seems to have inherited more active traits and all the negative energy of cynicism and fighting. Both his personal and literary life evidence this basic duality—dreaming of what could be, he fought earnestly against what was. In addition, *My Father's Son* uncovers a different sort of paternity. The two most compelling portraits in *My Father's Son* are of the two men who, after Corkery, may be said to have been O'Connor's literary fathers, Æ (George Russell) and W. B. Yeats. Though he does not directly say that Æ was like a father to him, O'Connor observes that the aging Russell always seemed to have looked on his "discoveries," writers like Colum and Kavanagh, as his sons. In fact, O'Connor suggests, "he developed something of the same possessiveness toward me."

About his relations with Yeats, O'Connor notes: "When he began to bully me I always gave him lip, almost on principle. After my father, I never quarrelled so much with anyone . . . . One might say that I was discovering my real father at last, and that all the old attitudes induced by my human father came on top." Despite his admitted devotion to Yeats, O'Connor is hardly gentle. "Yeats was a natural organizer, never happy unless organizing something or somebody—a great bully, as I discovered later, and an outrageous flatterer." O'Connor found it hard to comprehend the petty bickerings of Yeats and Æ, Yeats and Moore, Yeats and just about everyone. That O'Connor could treat his own literary idol with casual candor is just another indication of the sort of person he was.

One just doesn't call Yeats a "fathead," let alone a devious organizer. But then, one doesn't usually call Joyce "our greatest grammarian" either. That is, one doesn't say such things unless he happens to be Frank O'Connor.

"I saw life through a veil of literature." This statement in his autobiography defines something important about Frank O'Connor. After writing, reading was his most consuming activity. He read without method or grace, because he was both a writer and a self-taught person. Since he knew what he liked and disliked, he seldom hedged his bets. Thus, when he wrote about literature he often seemed too opinionated, too flamboyant. But as Richard Ellmann has noted, O'Connor "thought he was stating conclusions that nobody in his right mind could miss. The strength of *The Mirror in the Roadway* and *The Lonely Voice* comes from this assumptive power. It begins in close observation, of course, but then, in an almost visionary way, renders writers, objects and themes malleable." O'Connor didn't just read books, he collaborated with them.

Like everything else he wrote, O'Connor's "literary criticism" reveals as much about him as what he happens to be writing about. For instance, his short pamphlet, *The Art of the Theatre*, places great demands on everyone. Though he is writing from a writer's point of view, his radically inductive method imposes a sense of balance upon what he says. The whole of any work of art is indeed greater than the sum of its disparate parts. Collaboration is continuous and inconvenient creativity. Passivity on the part of an audience, abstraction or arrogance by the author, or virtuosity among the actors are all stifling to the theatre. For O'Connor a living moment in the theatre is no more or less significant than a moment of moments in a lyric poem or an epiphany in a story; that moment is a point, ephemeral at best and needful of continuous renewal. *The Art of the Theatre* is therefore not really literary criticism at all; it is creative opinion. O'Connor's literary biases are seldom hidden; he has no use for Art that imposes itself upon Reality, that constructs its forms *a priori*, or that assumes to enlighten belated races. The distinction between living and museum art appears over and over again in his writing. Academic or aesthetic literature plays to pure intellect in the rarefied atmosphere of the private soul. Instinctive or folk literature plays to impure emotions in the clamorous, unpredictable, and ultimately ephemeral world of the communal marketplace. In *The Road to Stratford*, for instance, he says, "Jonson was Joyce to Shakespeare's Yeats, the literary theorist as opposed to the natural instinctive writer."

"To have grown up in an Irish provincial town in the first quarter of the twentieth century," O'Connor writes at the beginning of *The Mirror in the Roadway*, "was to have known the nineteenth-century novel as a contemporary art form." As blazing as his round with the theatre was, it never approached the intensity of his intimate affair with the novel. His mentors in the art of fiction were not critics but novelists—Austen, Dickens, Chekhov, Flaubert, Trollope, and Joyce, to name a few. Like O'Connor's other "critical" books, *The Mirror in the Roadway* is audacious and uncompromising. He was not a critic viewing literature in a vacuum of abstraction, but a writer grubbing around with the dirty realities of writing. O'Connor's essays on individual novelists, above all else, reveal less concern with those abstractions generally taken as the "meaning" of novels than with why and how they wrote what they did. O'Connor was never quite able to consider literature in the vacuum of "pure art." Writers such as Balzac, Zola, and Trollope in his estimation struggled heroically with data, with the imposing form of the "objective" world of things, because "the times" demanded that the writer know the world he wrote about. The writers of the twentieth century in reaction to this imposition demanded that the reader know something. Proust, Joyce, Lawrence, and Faulkner quite naturally reversed the mirror and looked at the subjective side of life. "The tables are turned with a vengeance," O'Connor concludes.

The tension between object and subject that he considered so vital to Shakespeare's drama carries equal weight in O'Connor's conception of modern fiction. Recalling the question placed by a crafty theologian to Christ as to which was the most important commandment, O'Connor suggests that this insistent academic was posing the age-old conflict "between subjective and objective truth, between faith and good works . . . between symbolism and naturalism, communism and fascism." Christ's equivocal suggestion to love God *and* love thy neighbor represents in O'Connor's mind the irreducible ground of truth for the modern artist—namely, "that reality is inapprehensible; that if we keep our minds and hearts like clear glass, the light of God shines through us, but that we can be certain of God's presence within us only by the light it sheds on the world outside us. That, in fact, truth is subjective and objective, and that there is no truth

greater than this." O'Connor took literature seriously
and *The Mirror in the Roadway* stands, if for no other
reason, as a defense of literature.

O'Connor's opinions about drama and the novel are
those of a writer whose performances in those forms are
at best modest. However, his ideas on the short story
rest on a solid base of practice and accomplishment.
When he finally got around to writing critically about
the short story, he slipped into *apologia*, not just of the
genre but of his entire life as well. Admitting that he
was not all that sure what he meant by the term "short
story," O'Connor insisted that he was "passionately
clear" about what he did not mean. To him it was not
a yarn or a squib or, as E. M. Forster put it, a piece
of prose fiction of a certain length. Though it shares
with the novel a commitment to plausible reality, the
short story differs both in form and attitude from the
novel. Time, O'Connor suggested in "And It's a Lonely,
Personal Art," collaborates with the novelist to estab-
lish a rhythm of continuing life. "Time the gasbag," on
the other hand, is the enemy of the short-story writer,
who must locate that "glowing center of action from
which past and future will be equally visible." That
moment of crisis is the story, according to O'Connor.
The novel by contrast is the result of the entire process
of events. "The story, like the play," he writes in *The
Lonely Voice,* "must have the element of immediacy,
the theme must plummet to the bottom of the mind."

All in all, the main difference for Frank O'Connor
between the story and the novel is not so much formal
as ideological. The novel places man in society, "but
the short story remains by its very nature remote from
the community—romantic, individualistic, and intransi-

gent." Therefore, always "in short story there is this sense of outlawed figures wandering about the fringes of society, superimposed sometimes on symbolic figures whom they caricature and echo—Christ, Socrates, Moses." A recognition of defeat and the need to escape characterize "Gogal's officials, Turgenev's serfs, Maupassant's prostitutes, Chekhov's doctors and teachers, Sherwood Anderson's provincials." O'Connor himself admitted that this idea was shaky: "It is too vast for a writer with no critical or historical training to explore by his own inner light." Like most of his abstract notions it is extremely vulnerable and openended, but at least it fits his entire conception of life and literature and it is, above all, alive. Even more vibrant and worthy are his essays in *The Lonely Voice* on individual short-story writers, including Kipling, D. H. Lawrence, Isaac Babel, A. E. Coppard. By and large, the essays are terse and perceptive, almost devoid of modish critical jargon or narrow academic bias. What one hears in *The Lonely Voice* is one great writer of short fiction collaborating with other great writers of short fiction enthusiastically and honestly.

Undeniably, literature in all its various forms was O'Connor's playground. On the other hand, he was incapable of absolute escape; he was an Irish writer and Ireland was his battleground. Consequently, his most powerful critical opinions were about Irish writing. Few other writers or critics have written as well or as widely about Irish and Anglo-Irish literature as Frank O'Connor. Shortly after finishing *The Lonely Voice*, O'Connor turned his hand to the book suggested thirty years before by Yeats—a history of Irish literature. *The Backward Look*, as it was eventually called, is actually a criticism of a larger life, a synthesis of a culture, and a personal statement. O'Connor's "backward look," then, is every bit as personally telling as his autobiographies or his stories.

In the first half of *The Backward Look*, O'Connor the translator is at work, talking about Irish literature in Irish. His textual arguments, though based on thorough learning, have an intuitive flair that would make a professional scholar cringe. Yet his prosodic interpretations reveal an ear that any poet would envy. His own meticulous translations (in most cases accompanied by an Irish text) provide sturdy support for his speculations. In the second half of *The Backward Look* Frank O'Connor the Anglo-Irish writer holds forth on Irish literature in English. He constantly underscores the complex political forces that shaped Irish literature from Swift to Yeats. To his mind the first masterpiece written in English in Ireland was a political tract— Swift's *A Modest Proposal.* "That political note," he suggests, "is characteristic of all Anglo-Irish literature. I know no other literature so closely linked to the immediate reality of politics." The death of a literature in Irish was a political reality, the harsh result of Cromwell's devastations.

In the twentieth century the two Irish writers who stand out for O'Connor are Yeats and Joyce. He finds it significant that whereas Joyce saw in Charles Stewart Parnell something symbolic of Ireland's search for itself, Yeats looked instead to Cuchulain. The difference, according to O'Connor, is "part of an antithesis that was to develop in modern Irish literature between Yeats and Joyce, the idealist and the realist, the countryman and the townsman, the dead past and the unborn future." Needless to say, O'Connor spends more time on Yeats and Joyce than on any other writers in Ireland's literary history. His notion of their anti-thetical arrangement may be assailable but it is not at all limiting. For him an idea was a risk, a venture toward truthfulness rather than a static truth in itself. The antithesis between Yeats and Joyce, like his notion of the backward look, is less important for what it means than for what it does—it opens up concrete opportunities for O'Connor's restless intuitions.

If any single assumption or attitude dominates O'Connor's critical writing it is his wariness of the intellect. In *The Backward Look* he argues that a litera-ture heavy with political themes and oral techniques is necessarily a literature for "common readers" and not for the sophisticated. O'Connor was convinced that scholarship dries up the radical sources of poetry, that abstraction dulls the concrete impulses of the imagina-tion. His test for gauging Irish literature, and in fact all literature, was whether or not it produces "the shock of man's fundamental experience set down as though for the first time." That shock is primal and instinctive, not derivative or learned. The backward look, then, is also a forward impulse: coming to terms with what you are, you confront what you are becoming. To risk collaboration with Bryan Merryman or Swift, with Ferguson or Yeats, is to venture into a magical and improvising process.

2

A Provincial's Battle with Provincialism

Rather against prevailing opinion, O'Connor insisted that in spite of the "backward look" of its literature, "no nation in the world is so divorced from its own past as Ireland." The nineteenth century obliterated "every mark of cultural identity," leaving almost irreparable historical gaps. O'Connor considered it shameful, for instance, that despite the rhetoric of the government about the Irish language "thousands of students pass through our universities each year with less knowledge of their own culture than one would expect to find among American students." He found it ironic indeed that the revival of Irish "coincided with the emergence of a strong literature in English, and its rapid decline since the establishment of a native government with the official attempt at destroying Irish literature in English." Speaking from personal experience, he claimed that the "literature of the past is simply ignored; the literature of our own time is either ignored or banned by law. . . . As for our archaeological and architectural monuments, they scarcely bear thinking of."

Therefore, Frank O'Connor did battle not against but for Ireland, arguing that "we in Ireland can afford" to discard the past less than any other people "because without it we have nothing and we are nothing." However, O'Connor's earnest belief in the worth of Ireland's culture met both public apathy and official opposition. The backward look, while providing vital mythology and genuine emotion, had also become perverted by banal nostalgia and superficial nationalism. Just as his enthusiastic and audacious literary criticism bothered the fragile egos of academic critics, so his intense campaign to inform the Irish people of their past actually threatened those managing (perhaps mismanaging) Ireland's present. Though it was just another of the lost causes championed by Frank O'Connor, salvaging Ireland's past nevertheless produced three of his most imaginative improvisations— *Kings, Lords, & Commons*, *The Big Fellow*, and *Irish Miles*.

Apart from the short story, no other activity absorbed O'Connor's interest more steadily than the translation of Irish poetry into English. His tireless efforts carried no motive of gain or self-aggrandizement. His scholarship, admittedly improvised, was simply an avocation. According to D. A. Binchy, O'Connor was a "scholar-gipsy," who left professionals amazed by his intuition, which "after a number of wildly false starts," usually produced the right translation. He was fortunate to have many scholarly friends: Corkery in his youth, Bergin during the early Dublin years, Binchy and Greene later on. In these relationships he exploited the creative tension between knowing and doing. The main problem for O'Connor was not to know exactly what the poet meant, but "how to give the reader the feeling that he 'was there.'" He believed that there is in most Irish

folk poetry "an element of ingenuousness, even of
clumsiness, which the academic translator in his
laudable desire to attach his poem to the corpus of
accepted poetry tends to gloss over, forgetting that it is
the acceptance of this very awkwardness which so often
established a poem in the general mind." Defending
the disproportionate number of translations by O'Connor in his *Love Poems of the Irish*, Sean Lucy claims
that O'Connor, "more than any other, has done for
this generation what Hyde and Ferguson did for theirs."

In *Kings, Lords, & Commons* O'Connor brought
together poems from three decades of translating,
poems published in *The Wild Bird's Nest*, *Lords and
Commons*, and *The Fountain of Magic*. It is a complete
and mature offering by a poet of considerable power
and imagination. As wild and exuberant as some of the
translations appear, especially next to those of other
translators, neither the voice declaiming nor the personality revealed is that of O'Connor. If not always faithful
to the literal meaning, at least he was always faithful
to the tone of the voice.

The very impressive first part of *Kings, Lords, &
Commons* offers poems from the hermitages and
monasteries of medieval Ireland. Some are religious
poems celebrating Christ and some are court poems
honoring heroes of the pagan sagas. Some evoke
nature in stylized metric conventions and some bring
forth those "revenant" figures who have "escaped
death only to return and find that Ireland, under
the Christians, has gone to Hell."

One particularly nice nature poem is "The Blackbird
at Belfast Lough." I quote both original and Gerard
Murphy's prose translation from *Early Irish Lyrics*:

Int én bec	The little bird which has
re léic feit	whistled from the end of a
de rinn guip	bright-yellow bill:
glanbuidi:	it utters a note above Belfast
fo-ceird faid	Loch—from a yellow-heaped
ós Loch Laíg,	branch.
lon do chraíb	
charnbuidi.	

O'Connor's verse translation preserves both the distinctive metrical shape and the lyrical mood:

> What little throat
> Has framed that note?
> What gold beak shot
>   It far away?
> A blackbird on
> His leafy throne
> Tossed it alone
>   Across the bay.

That is precise and evocative poetry with nothing superfluous either to sound or to sense.

The best Irish poetry emanates from the vigor and immediacy of its primitive drama. O'Connor found himself perfectly at home with the dramatic monologues that abound in Irish poetry, among the finest of which is "Liadain." Having failed in a test of her virtue, Liadain is heard lamenting the loss of Cuirithir:

> Gain without gladness
>   Is in the bargain I have struck:
> One that I loved I wrought to madness.
>
> Mad without measure
>   But for God's fear that numbed her heart
> She would not do his pleasure.

In the sixth stanza Liadain is heard to say:

> Woods woke
>   About us for a lullaby
> And the blue waves in music spoke.

O'Connor, taking slight liberties with the original, has quietly accented the love of the pair; the woods do not sing just to her but to them both, together. O'Connor's version releases the drama of the entire situation by forcing the impact of severance and by personifying the effects of nature.

O'Connor revised nearly everything he wrote, even his translations. Nowhere is this penchant for tinkering more apparent than in "The Old Woman of Beare." As with his stories, each revision of this poem carried him closer to the dramatic crisis, closer to that glowing center of action. When it first appeared in Yeats's *Oxford Book of Modern Verse* (1936), it was a simple lyric, after the prevailing view of Kuno Meyer. By the time it showed up again in *Kings, Lords, & Commons,* three decades later, it had become a highly dramatic poem, in line with O'Connor's own notion that it was really part of a fuller romance about the Old Woman and St. Cummine. When the poem opens the old woman, now a nun, is heard lamenting her age:

> I, the old woman of Beare
> Once a shining shift would wear,
> Now and since my beauty's fall
> I have scarce a shift at all.

Her sensuality is coarse and frank, reminding one readily of Yeats's Crazy Jane. No remorse, no pious confession for past pleasures, just a faint wish that she could still enjoy them. In the end, O'Connor locates in the old woman's voice hesitant resignation:

> Floodtide!
> Flood or ebb upon the strand!
> What the floodtide brings to you
> Ebbtide carries from my hand.

It is a fine poem and O'Connor has done it justice.

In the second section of *Kings, Lords, & Commons* O'Connor presents some little-known poems by aristocratic court poets of the violent time in Irish history roughly parallel to the English Renaissance. The final section of the volume *Peasants and Dreamers* overlaps that epoch somewhat in time but not in sentiment. In these poems from the sixteenth to the eighteenth century a distinct sense of national identity surfaces. In "Sarsfield," which O'Connor considered the first democratic poem in Irish, one encounters such quatrains as this:

> I'll climb the mountain a lonely man,
> And I'll go east again if I can,
> 'Twas there I saw the Irish ready for the fight,
> The lousy crowd that wouldn't unite!

"Kilcash" is a political variation of the *ubi sunt* motif. In it a faceless voice of the Irish people laments the destruction of the forests of Ireland by English armies in search of Sarsfield's armies. The opening inquiry is sincere and forceful:

What shall we do for timber?
The last of the woods is down.
Kilcash and the home of its glory
And the bell of the house are gone. . . .

Suffering in the poem is communal suffering; the forests belonged, after all, to the people. Natural erosion or the decay of time can be accepted with stoic resignation, but ruthless tyranny deserves the kind of fervent and partisan tone which pervades the poem.

The longest, the most impressive, and indeed the most famous (if you will, infamous) poem in *Kings, Lords, & Commons* is "The Midnight Court." In his introduction O'Connor notes that when Merriman "died in 1805 in a house on Clare Street, Limerick, Irish literature in the Irish language may be said to have died with him." O'Connor's translation was banned. That Merriman's Irish original had never been banned suggests that ecclesiastical and political pietists either did not or could not read the official language of the Irish Republic. O'Connor observed with a wink: "I believe that the best authorities hold that it is almost entirely my own work, the one compliment Ireland ever paid me." O'Connor translated "The Midnight Court" almost as if he had written the original himself simply because of his rare gift for collaborating with the past. Merriman's *Cúirt an Mheadhán Oichche* possesses the style and wit of eighteenth-century England along with the candor and gusto of its folk past. There is a good deal of Pope and Burns in the poem, perhaps even of Chaucer and Rabelais. This translation also reveals something of Frank O'Connor—the contentious spirit, the irreverence, the desire for naturalness, and the commitment to freedom.

Structured somewhat in the manner of medieval dream romances, "The Midnight Court" is carried by simple and conventional narrative devices. On a serene walk one morning an old man stops for a rest and falls asleep. In his dream an ugly hag escorts him to a fairy court. The plaintiff is a young woman, upset by the lack of available men in Ireland; the defendant is a bitter old man, driven to misogyny by an unfortunate marriage. The woman pleads:

> Wouldn't you think I must be a fright,
> To be shelved before I get started right;
> Heartsick, bitter, dour and wan,
> Unable to sleep for the want of a man?

The old man declaims venomously, attacking her pedigree and her social station, and resorting finally to the time-honored Christian position that evil entered human affairs through woman.

The girl counters by imagining the old man in bed with his young bride:

> You'd all agree 'twas a terrible fate
> Sixty winters on his pate,
> A starved old gelding, blind and lamed
> And a twenty year old with her parts untamed.

That O'Connor enjoyed himself with the poem is obvious. His couplets strain for the rhyme now and then, and he does not always match the sonority of the original. Yet beyond the theme of sexual freedom, a more serious notion is apparent in O'Connor's translation. Sexual impotence is part of a greater bondage, and the need for love is part of a "great hunger," the hunger for genuine freedom. Obviously, what Bryan

Merriman saw in eighteenth-century Ireland was not
much different from what O'Connor saw in twentieth-
century Ireland.

Considering his own strong opinions together with
the weight of politics in Irish literature, it is hardly
surprising that O'Connor wrote at least one book on a
strictly political subject. Since O'Connor had himself
opposed the treaty engineered by Collins and Griffith,
the appearance in 1937 of *The Big Fellow*: *Michael
Collins and the Irish Revolution* caused more than a
little consternation in Dublin. The Irish Republic was
then in its second decade of existence. Men like O'Connor, disillusioned by the home-grown tyranny of de
Valera's party, felt that the heat of genius had been
replaced by the "cold touch of normality." They
suspected that the "day of lofty ideals was over."
So O'Connor wrote a biography of Michael Collins,
perhaps the one man most responsible for the success
of the Irish Revolution.

O'Connor looks primarily at those six intense years
which were for Collins and the Irish people eternal
moments of identification. Not stopping to ponder
whether men make history or history men, O'Connor
suggests that the Revolution and Collins were practical-
ly the same thing. Though the manner of the book is
anecdotal and impressionistic, O'Connor adheres strictly to the facts. His research has been so uncompro-
misingly assimilated that objectivity and subjectivity
merge. O'Connor had himself been part of the Revolution; he even served time for his obstinate refusal to
recognize the treaty to end it. Likewise, he is part of
his story about it, if satire can be called participation.

The satiric tone of *The Big Fellow* is apparent from

the outset. The opening chapter is called "Lilliput in London." Collins is cast as a man set apart, by size and by talent, from Lilliput. The narrative breaks stride only to contrast the big fellow with all the little fellows. Despite the glaring difference, O'Connor presents Collins not so much as a rarefied deity but as a brutally impetuous human being with ambivalent motives. What O'Connor saw apparently was a guerrilla fighter, not a revolutionist fighting for his own political powers, but an ontological rebel saying "no" to tyranny in general.

The first section of the book covers Collins's rise to prominence after the Easter Rising to September 1919. The second section, *The Body and the Lash,* concerns his role in the guerrilla war which ended in a stalemate in the summer of 1921. The final section captures Collins's *Tragic Dilemma* in the sticky negotiations with Britain; and, as O'Connor builds toward the murder of Collins shortly after ratification of the treaty, his satiric edge gives way to a loftier tone. Collins died by a Republican bullet near his home in County Cork. "The countryside he had seen in dreams, the people he had loved, the tradition which had been his inspiration—they had risen in the fallen light and struck him dead." The deaths of Collins and Griffith destroyed Sinn Fein and with it the hopes of O'Connor's generation.

> It destroyed the prospect which, we are only just beginning to realise, Collins' life opened up: fifteen years—perhaps more, perhaps less—of hard work, experiment, enthusiasm; all that tumult and pride which comes of the leadership of a man of genius who embodies the best in a nation.

For O'Connor the most pressing tragedy is that in the end life returns to normal, almost as if genius had never

ventured through at all. But for some, O'Connor
especially, "Collins had spoiled them for lesser men."

O'Connor's perennial struggle with Irish provincialism is most obvious in his one-man campaign to preserve that unique Irish heritage held so precariously in
the monasteries, castles, big houses, and megalithic
sites scattered about Ireland. Needless to say, he took
up the cause with ferocity. The first skirmishes appeared
appropriately in *The Bell* in 1942. More articles appeared
in *The Irish Times*, all with the same fervor. Even
sharper statements came in a series of articles for the
Sunday Independent (March 1943 to September 1945),
published under the pseudonym "Ben Mayo." *Irish
Miles* (1947) represents the culmination of O'Connor's
campaign and the best of his so-called Irish travel
books. Though about his travels in Ireland, *Irish Miles*
is a travel book only as *The Big Fellow* is biography.
It is closer to Synge's *The Aran Islands* than, for instance,
O'Faolin's *An Irish Journey*, a charming, even "racy"
book that reveals little about the man himself. In *Irish
Miles* O'Connor is always himself—effusive and restless,
lyrical and irascible.

The campaign to preserve Irish architecture obtrudes
from time to time, usually as wry sarcasm directed at
negligent officials. On finding another fine house gutted
by "housebreakers" O'Connor notes: "Why on earth
any Irish government should imagine that Ireland
hadn't ruins enough and that it was their duty to fill
it with more, I didn't understand, but then there is a
lot about Irish governments which I don't understand."
At Cashel he comments that "the great mass of build-
ings in which the whole history of Ireland is concentrated, abandoned by both Churches, exists only on the

grudging charity of the Commissioners of the Public Works." This indignation derives, however, not from political doctrine but from aesthetic and cultural integrity.

What O'Connor saw was a unique civilization being chipped away by petty partisans who possessed no sense of Ireland's past and a severely limited vision of its future. Kilmallock, for instance, the home of Desmond as well as of de Valera, elicits this sharp blast:

> The Fitzgerald tombs rot under the open sky within the parish church while the Protestants repair to their new church on the hill, the Catholics to their grand Gothic church; and all of them, the last of their historic houses demolished, to see Hollywood films in a cinema called after Patrick Sarsfield. One glance at that dying hole, and you can understand the dreariest of Mr. De Valera's political manifestos. With a synthetic religion and a synthetic culture, what is there left but abstractions?

But inevitably O'Connor's love of Ireland is as passionate as his indignation; sarcasm is usually tempered by human balance. "Life is too short," he says, "to discover the reason for all the ruins in Ireland."

Throughout the book O'Connor manages to make culture a living story in which the artifacts of a people are the people themselves. Moving on ground level at cycling pace, literally and figuratively, O'Connor noses his way around Ireland looking at stone structures, listening to people talk, and finding in the end the living substance of his art. His narrative moves at the same pace and follows this "respectable middle-aged writer with his wife and friend" from the Boyne Valley south through Leinster, west through Munster and north through Connaught.

If O'Connor is right and "civilization is merely a matter of communications," then Ireland is, or at least was, civilized. Every abbey, every mountain, every village communicates something. Atop Cashel's Rock, for instance, O'Connor grasps momentarily the mystery of Cormac's Chapel. Inside, the rain, dripping through windows broken since Tudor times, has eaten away the carved heads and coated the walls with a "thick layer of green, phosphorescent slime." The arcading is barely visible in the "green subaqueous light" that casts gloom on the cavelike room. To O'Connor this represented "European art with a vengeance."

Though it is the people that fascinate O'Connor, the book hardly lacks in scenic description. In fact, it contains some of his most impressive descriptive writing. In a characteristic passage he describes how "The country mounted on either side of us in bleak grey hills; gradually it came closer to the road, all choppy like a sea, threatening it here and there in bumpty, grassy hillocks, till all at once, as we reached the top of the hill and began our free-wheel down into Inchigeela, it rose and hurled itself on us, snapping at us with red sandstone teeth between purple lips of heather." O'Connor can picture in equally vivid and unself-conscious language a sunset over the Clare hills or the grey pallor of Connemara or a bitter wind at Tralee. It's just that Nature, though well enough in its own way, "produces a ravenous appetite for civilization." The irony is that civilization, at least that encountered by these cyclists, proves to be not altogether satisfying either.

Through it all, the persistent personality of the writer

himself controls *Irish Miles*. One gets the impression
not just of a voice speaking but of eyes seeing, ears
listening, and a nose smelling. For that matter, everything he experiences and everyone he contacts, including
his cycling companions, come to life. Célimène, for
instance, shows an extraordinary capacity to handle
patiently all the whims and outbursts of her exuberant
but irritable husband. Moreover, she tends to indulge a
kind of Gothic fantasy from time to time by insisting
on the possibility of ghosts. After a particularly bad
night at a certain hotel, the narrator reasons that it
was not because of ghosts "but because though Célimène is a very nice girl, she did not go with the architecture. Greta Garbo and myself would have had a lovely
time." That's the voice of a man dreaming.

O'Connor's ambivalent attachment to his native
Cork reveals itself when Célimène forces him not to
bypass the city. "I had to explain to her as well as I
could that a writer who goes back to his native place
is rather in the position of Heine's monkey chewing his
tail. Objectively he is eating, subjectively he is being
eaten." But only a few miles outside Cork nostalgic
memories sneak through, especially in the account of
the delightful visit to Gougane Barre and Tim Buckley,
the Tailor. After listening to a magical tale of a one-
legged priest and his bout with the fairies, the cyclists
prepare to leave but find the door barricaded by a tree
stump—nothing more than persecution from local
pietists over the banned book, *The Tailor and Ansty*.
O'Connor concludes: "Going back over the hill I
could feel like an actual physical presence the sense of
evil in the valley." He may well have added with all the
humor of a disillusioned humanist the comment he

saves until the end of the book. Somewhere near O'Briensbridge they encounter a poster picture of the Icilma lass "with a modesty vest of brown paper pasted across her pretty chest! 'Civilization?' I thought, going cold all over. 'Did I say civilization?'"

By his vigorous campaigns to salvage Ireland's past, O'Connor established himself as Ireland's slightly abrasive conscience. The same exasperated attachment to Ireland is evident in O'Connor's fiction, particularly his two novels. Both *The Saint and Mary Kate* and *Dutch Interior* were groping attempts not only of a writer for a suitable form but also of an Irishman for a cohesive consciousness. In them he was seriously confronting himself and his past; for O'Connor to do battle with the provincial narrowness of Cork was to attack his own provincialism. He once said that Ireland always looked out on the world through windows and doors. That notion, to a great extent, defines what O'Connor was trying to do in his novels. The two young people in *The Saint and Mary Kate* look outward from a Cork slum tenement toward the freedom and light of the outside world. The young people of *Dutch Interior* continually escape from respectable homes and jobs into darkened Cork streets and peer back through windows and doors, hoping to find warmth and life. Significantly, the doors are closed and the windows are heavily curtained.

The Saint and Mary Kate is about two radically different young people and their attempt to move from the restrictions of poverty to a larger world outside. It is what O'Connor referred to as a "tragedy of innocence." Mary Kate McCormick and Phil Dinan are products of a Cork tenement called the Doll's House.

Mary Kate, the illegitimate daughter of the tenement's "loose woman," is one of those people for whom even the Cork quays are "magical miles." The intensity of her longing takes various forms, but generally it is an inchoate desire for "something else." Phil, on the other hand, is a model of piety and self-control. He has "that complete disregard of worldly appearance that belongs to a saint." He is also obsessed by the clock. Every morning, for instance, he and Mary Kate attend Mass to pray for his dying mother. When Mary Kate oversleeps one morning, Phil refuses to call again unless she attaches a note to her door each morning explicitly stating her intention to accompany him to Mass. He has even counted the steps between the Doll's House and the church. On the unlikely affinity of these two "innocents" the novel turns.

As compelling and sensitive as it is, *The Saint and Mary Kate* is not a successful novel. On the one hand, O'Connor takes an abstraction too seriously and lets it dictate his characters. That is generally a weakness for a novelist. For a storyteller like O'Connor it is disastrous. The particular abstraction is the opposition between two conflicting ways of life, represented by Mary Kate, "Eternal Woman," and Phil, "Eternal Boy." The idea obviously plagued O'Connor, because it appeared so often and in so many forms in his later work. On the other hand, to O'Connor's credit perhaps, he is too easily diverted from his deterministic "tragedy of innocence." He appears so intrigued by the hero and heroine that he barely elaborates on the world in which they live, the world that supposedly crushes their dreams. By his own critical standards, though, a novel requires a society, not just a vague backdrop. O'Connor's

inclinations as a storyteller get in the way. Even when
he sketches a tenement feud, a striking face, or an
overheard comment, it is almost an aside, a passing
glance toward a momentary scene, rather than part
of a carefully sustained totality. All in all, then, the part
dominates the whole in *The Saint and Mary Kate*.

In *Dutch Interior*, O'Connor ostensibly turned that
corner, perhaps with a vengeance. Being too close to the
issue (once again a vaguely deterministic notion of
people trapped by their environment), he sought detachment by way of technique. The impressionistic
form, which really appears formless, is calculated to
present a tapestry meaningful only in a large scale.
The narrative, such as it is, develops from the static,
suffocating atmosphere of a city, rather than from the
motion of people's lives. The emptiness of the characters
of *Dutch Interior* is the emptiness of the world of things
that surround them—streets, clocks, churches, shops,
and walls. The characters are not much more than symp-
toms of a diseased society. They are acted on almost
solely from without. One is, in fact, meant to be less
interested in the characters than in what has trapped
them. The silhouettes of passengers seen by Peter
Devane, for instance, through the portholes and doorways of a newly arrived steamer almost exactly equal
what O'Connor allows us to see of his characters—
vague silhouettes.

However, that's precisely the point. In the routines
of the city, life has become vague and ghostly. Even
the young people have been so deadened by things and
customs that they are only shadows. Concealed figures
caress in dark doorways and hollow laughter seeps from
the shadows, but a "silence within doors" suggests

loneliness and emptiness. Stevie Dalton stands in the twilight after work admiring from afar the house of "The Beautiful Miss Maddens"; "after dark when the whole house was lit up he would stand at the gate and glower at it." Gus Devane and his friend stand idly watching folks on the passing trams. They are all what O'Connor called in an unpublished novel written toward the end of his life, "displaced persons."

The effect of the persistent piling of one sterile routine on another is a "claustrophobia which only violence could shatter." However, O'Connor allows no violence—that romantic ideal ended with the Civil War. The only other recourse for his characters is flight. Gus, "the eternal Quixote," leaves for America after being caught with a prostitute. The Madden girls flee into loveless marriages and one eventually to an asylum. Peter and Stevie are part of the "ghostly file" who remain. They are silhouettes as well, suspended in "Time's Pocket" because in "ten years' time it will make no difference to anyone in the world." There are no more rebels, only survivors. The book ends with ghosts, those imprecise abstractions of the past and an empty room, extending like a "Dutch interior" into nothing.

Dutch Interior is richly impressionistic, but probably too full, too undisciplined to strike clear. It contains some of O'Connor's most lyrical prose. A reviewer called one of his plays a "novelist's play." *Dutch Interior* could be called a "poet's novel." But without a discernible voice to unify the images or to focus the drama, the novel lacks a sure emotional perspective. O'Connor's alienation from the piety, respectability, and half truth of his provincial past is too close to the surface, too unrefined. Furthermore, O'Connor appears unable to sustain a narrative about the blighted lives of two brothers without indulging quick glances toward the other lives they cross. The finest portions of the book, especially those concerning Eileen Madden, are almost diversionary, the subject perhaps of another novel. As a result, the larger tapestry is weakened, though it is in the whole that O'Connor has invested his cumulative effect.

Dutch Interior, as well as *The Saint and Mary Kate,* illustrates O'Connor's strengths as clearly as his weaknesses. He was a lyric poet who felt ill at ease behind the mannered mask of Poetry. He was a storyteller interested more in the flash points of human existence than in the sweeping artifice. A novel traces human life on a sustained line in time and space; a story locates a singular, irreducible point. The formal demands of the one, extension and duration, are distinct from those of the other, immediacy and clarity. The sense of containment, of closed energy, that characterizes O'Connor's stories is precisely what hinders the progressive and differentiating strategy of the novel.

As flawed as they are, the novels deal with the issues that pepper all of O'Connor's writing—the incrustation of Irish life, the capacity of people to dream and to delude themselves, the failure of domestic relations as well as all institutions to provide love and genuineness, and above all, the pervasive burden of human loneliness. Then too, the characters of the novels are about the same as those one finds in the stories—little people, anonymous flecks of humanity, innocents, and outcasts. The novels also manifest the main traits of O'Connor's simple style. The prose is unpretentious,

with no trace of literary allusion or intellectual orna-
mentation. The narrative is compact, carried not by
exposition but by intense and brisk dialogue. But
above all, the novels go a long way toward explaining
why O'Connor inevitably stayed with the short story.

3

A Lonely, Personal Art

A short story is a singular thing, often tucked away in a magazine among essays, poems, and reviews without the comfort of a dozen or so more by the same author. O'Connor wrote almost two hundred stories and published them in such scattered places as *The Irish Statesman, Lovatt Dickenson Magazine, The Bell, Harper's Bazaar,* and *The Atlantic Monthly.* Following the enthusiastic reception of "Guests of the Nation," he accepted the offer of Macmillan Ltd. to publish a collection of stories under that title. Over the four decades of his writing career, he put together seven of these major collections, each made up of recently published stories. His files and manuscripts indicate that he revised and ordered the stories for these collections very meticulously, seeking as he said not artificial unity but some approximation of "ideal ambiance." The collections (he also made some selected editions) were not just warmed-over toast to draw a few extra quid; they were serious literary ventures. To consider some of these collections in this brief study is, then, not only convenient but quite reasonable. I have chosen to consider one volume from each of the decades of his career. This regrettably excludes discussion of some of the most famous stories, namely "Guests of the Nation," "My Oedipus Complex," and "The Drunkard." But I trust it will provide some hint of the larger picture of O'Connor's "lonely, personal art" as well as allow for a close look at some of the finer details of his mastery of this rather limited and demanding genre.

The stories of *Bones of Contention* are typical of O'Connor's writing in the 1930s. By his own admission he was "fumbling for a style." Having found the exuberant romanticism of *Guests of the Nation* unproductive, he drew back his sights from the nation at large to smaller and less colorful social groups. The characters of these stories are not soldiers or lovers; they are peasants, drunken musicians, and tired old men. The narrative voice is casual and direct, calling attention to the persons in the story rather than to itself. Such phrases as "for as the old man said to me of him," or "as they all said," create in the story "Peasants," for example, the impression of a story overheard, almost like gossip, from the peasants themselves about the "unpleasant memories" left behind by a former priest. "Orpheus and His Lute," the hilarious account of the drinking habits of the Irishtown Brass and Reed Band, is told entirely as a *shanachie* tale. In fact, when O'Connor read many of these stories over the radio, they proved immensely popular. They contained enough of what the Tailor called "marvels" to keep folks awake. For a writer so young these stories are surprisingly trim in form. What moral "comment" there is emerges from a natural and mature balancing of sympathy and judgment.

Though by no means its best story, the title story is indicative of the prevailing manner of the entire volume. The very phrase "bones of contention," suggests low-grade dissension, not revolution; the struggles within all of the stories are, for the most part, isolated, petty, and spontaneous. Set in Cork and narrated by the grandson of the central figure, "Bones of Contention" concerns the monumental and eminently funny feud that erupts when a stubborn, hard-drinking, opinionated old woman insists upon supervising the funeral of an old friend. The cliché title serves as ironic comment on the whole affair, for it is over a corpse that the "battle" is waged. The triviality of it all does not diminish the intensity of the conflict, so that all the fiery words and contentious bitching serve only to upset a normally serene community. The same kind of verbal battling appears as well in the next story, "What's Wrong With the Country?" Listening to the rather senseless and astonishingly prolix debate, one can't help thinking of Joxer and Captain Boyle in *Juno and the Paycock* lamenting the great "chassis" abroad in the world. One concludes, not altogether without the assistance of a slightly irascible narrator, that *talk* is what's wrong with the country.

A number of stories in *Bones of Contention* reveal the curious notions held by Irish villagers and townsfolk about the law. What O'Connor seems to be testing is the casual attitude taken by tightly knit social groups to any formal system of national law. The disparity between a provincial community's internal strife and its unified opposition to external control is given delightfully comic treatment by O'Connor in "Peasants." The terrible burden of communal guilt is the subject of "In the Train," though it takes most of the story for the tragic predicament to unfold. O'Connor's technical problem in the story is to capture the drama of a murder trial without using the customary context of the court. After all, people live and die outside the courts. So O'Connor pushes the reader momentarily in a false direction by presenting a train full of assorted people—a chattering woman, her staid husband, his fellow policemen, a boisterous drunk, and a group of peasants described collectively as "gnarled, wild, with turbulent faces, their ill-cut clothes full of character." Discord between the sergeant and his busy wife lends an uneasy quality to the rather comic scene. The uneasiness assumes a darker tone with the conspicuous arrival of a "young woman in a brown shawl." The dialogue, so dramatic one can easily understand the story's successful stage adaptation, gradually reveals that most of the folks in the train have just come from this woman's trial.

Though foremost in everyone's mind, the woman, her crime, and the trial are skirted in the conversations. The policemen swap stories. The peasants converse about the weather or domestic cares. Without turning his attention directly on the woman herself, O'Connor gradually brings the chief business of the story into play. An old man suggests grimly that for the woman to return to Farranchreesht is a "great impudence." Someone else avows that "no one could ever darken her door again." Yet all of them have testified in her favor at the trial. "There was never an informer in my family," says one. Her guilt is a certainty to them, but they refuse to allow the law to meddle in a community affair. If she is to be punished, then it should be by her neighbors, not by some abstract system administered by strangers in the city.

Finally, O'Connor turns directly to the woman, exploring her thoughts about the trial. The silent pathos of her loneliness began the moment of her acquittal. As the train nears its destination the story quickens. The policemen offer sarcastic congratulations. " 'The law is truly a remarkable phenomenon,' said the sergeant, who was also rather squiffy. 'Here you are, sitting at your ease at the expense of the State, and for one word, one simple word of a couple of letters, you could be lying in the body of the gaol, waiting for the rope and the morning jaunt.' " Neither the peasants nor the policemen evoke sympathy; they are judged by their own contradictory ethic. But then, neither is the young woman portrayed as spotless. In a masterful stroke, O'Connor concludes with a startling suggestion of motive. Magner, the most repulsive of the policemen and the one whose drunken remarks reveal the most venom, addresses the woman by her name and announces, "There'll be one happy man in Farranchreesht to-night." The common rumor is that Helena killed her miserly husband for Cady Driscoll. Her adamant denial alone raises some doubt: " 'No more to me,' she repeated dully to her own image in the window, 'no more to me than the salt sea!' " The story ends suspended; knowledge is as tentative as the law is arbitrary.

"The Majesty of the Law," in contrast to "In the Train," is a comic but equally dramatic rendering of O'Connor's conviction that "abstract considerations like justice, truth and personal integrity melt before the personal element." By this he meant that the lofty irrelevance, the uniformed majesty, of the law is precisely the reason for its impotence. At best the law only arrests human conflict temporarily; it never resolves conflict once and for all. And at worst, the law actually can complicate conflict, widen the gaps between people. For too long Ireland was occupied by a police force more or less removed from the people. The sergeant of "The Majesty of the Law," and the policemen of "In the Train," are caught between public position and private integrity in performing their "duty." Either way objectivity is inhumane and subjectivity is risky. "So what's majestic about the law?" we wonder.

Old Dan Bride, the petty felon of the story, appears as a person totally in harmony with his surroundings. The visit of the sergeant upsets his deliberate life hardly at all. Instead the two men fall naturally into casual conversation. An "easy posture" is maintained by tea and pipes. Convention prevails and the story settles into rituals of hospitality. The serenity of the situation disarms the reader. It's all too cordial; the rituals don't make sense because the reason for the sergeant's visit is unclear. The calm sharing of poteen creates a slight uneasiness. The sergeant conceals "whatever qualms he might have felt at the thought of imbibing illegal whiskey," and listens politely to Dan's discourse upon the art of making whiskey. His guarded tone suggests that the legal restrictions have destroyed ancient ways. They agree that it was probably a mistake for the law "to set its hand against" whiskey.

The passage of time goes unnoticed until at twilight the sergeant rises to leave. Halfway to the gate he turns almost in afterthought and casually intones, "I don't suppose you're thinking of paying that little fine, Dan?" Things fall into place. The petty rituals make sense: they have cemented personal contact, while delaying official business. The sergeant now can legitimately suggest that Dan come to serve his sentence at his own convenience. Indeed, he has come with the expectation that Dan would refuse to buckle to the majesty of the law, that he would go to jail rather than pay a fine. In this way Dan actually transfers the sanctions of the community upon his accuser, who has broken the "personal element." By falling back on an archaic code of retribution, Dan Bride widens the gap between the abstract legal system and the conventions of the tribe. Consequently O'Connor has cut the personal element two ways, balancing our sympathy for Dan's civility and our judgment of his spiteful vindictiveness.

The instinctive wisdom of the conventions governing provincial Irish life seems to stem from the "backward look." The ancient ways of resolving tension are remnants of a way of life at once civilized and barbaric. O'Connor is neither nostalgic about these remnants nor terribly impressed by their modern replacements. In fact, there may even have been something subversive about these stories, the faint suggestion that Ireland's government was failing simply because it was betraying the people by indulging abstractions and disavowing the personal touch. But O'Connor's struggle in *Bones of Contention* is primarily with himself, a struggle for a suitable style and for genuine concerns.

The finest single story in *Bones of Contention*, "Michael's Wife," contains no provincial edginess or verbal squabbling. Irony is noticeably quiet and, above all, the sense of occasion is carried by highly evocative description. In his best stories O'Connor provides just enough physical background to give a particular incident locality. Dan Bride, the old man of "Majesty of the Law," fits securely into his rough-hewn, almost archaic environment. Helena, the felon of "In the Train," is placed in momentary relief by the description of Farranchreesht. The sense of total occasion crystallizes both stories, completing for a hesitant instant the incomplete puzzle of life. "Michael's Wife" is like the dramatic lyrics of ancient Irish poetry because of the way O'Connor merges the presentation of Irish place with the drama of an Irish person. It is not lyrical, as some critics have argued, just because of the descriptive language. It is lyrical because the sound of the voice is heard within a supremely resonant environment. And it is dramatic because its occasion is so immediate that the voice is at once discreet and expansive.

"Michael's Wife" is probably the most perfect il-lustration of O'Connor's theory of collaboration. In it he does indeed grab the reader by the lapels, dragging him into the center of the story. O'Connor himself sum-marizes the "bony structure" of the story in this way:

> We were down on the south coast of Ireland for a holiday and we got talkin' to this old farmer and he said his son, who was dead now, had gone to America. He'd married an American girl and she had come over for a visit, alone. Ap-parently her doctor had told her a trip to Ireland would do her good. And she stayed with the parents, had gone around to see his friends and other relations, and it wasn't till after she'd gone that they learned that the boy had died. Why didn't she tell them? There's your story.

O'Connor's center of attention is Michael's father, Tom Shea, whose center of attention is Michael's wife. The emptiness of the station where Tom meets the girl offers the first clue to the personal agonies of the characters. Her greeting, moreover, is a bit too warm. Weakened from travel and recent surgery, she is put immediately into Michael's room. Tom's wife, Maire, asks the ques-tion for us—why is she traveling? The girl is obviously out of place. The questions put to her are polite but honest; her answers are evasive. The reader gropes through the incisive dialogue for some thread of insight. "What's wrong?" we ask. "Why indeed is she here?" In other words, what is the occasion?

Tom floats in and out of our range of vision in a sort of muddled quandary. He alone hears the girl's groans and her weeping at night. Unable to verbalize his fear, Tom must suffer through the crisis. The morning of her departure, the girl is radiant, a shift in mood so brilliantly wrought by O'Connor as to bring the narrative to a crystallized conclusion without any expository revelation. To Maire's sober remark of farewell, "I know Michael is in good hands," the girl replies with a smile, "Yes, he is." No other word is spoken. Tom's fear, however, becomes terror as he drives her through the rain to the station.

> When he stood before the carriage door he looked at her appealingly. He could not frame the question he looked; it was a folly he felt must pass from him unspoken; so he asked only with his eyes, and with her eyes she answered him—a look of ecstatic fulfilment.

The train whistle speaks. His son's death is only as tacitly evident to us as it is to him. The burden of such supremely personal knowledge is awesome.

> He raised his hands to his eyes and swayed to and fro, moaning softly to himself. For a long time he remained like that, a ridiculous figure with the old potato bag and the little pool of water that gradually gathered on the platform about his feet.

Here is O'Connor's lonely voice. Tom Shea is ridiculously inarticulate, but he is also eminently human. The occasion bears with sufficient surety O'Connor's "comment" on those instinctively sensible ways in which people communicate the incommunicable and touch shared humanity.

As satisfying as it is, *Bones of Contention* is more or less of a piece. By the time he produced his third volume of stories O'Connor had not only explored the limits of his medium but had begun to expand them. The stories of the late thirties and early forties, many of which were originally published in *The Bell,* are consistently fine. Consequently, *Crab Apple Jelly,* published in 1944, is at once the most varied and the most disciplined single volume he was to produce. As its title implies, the volume is both sweet and tart, entertaining and serious. It contains some of the savage criticism of Irish life apparent in *Dutch Interior*; O'Connor was adamant that Ireland begin to look beyond its own shoreline. However, he does not cast blame or seek causes. His humanism accepts people for what they are. If there is a unity in the volume it is not a preconceived campaign, just a natural unity of manner and tone.

The first story, "Bridal Night," is powerfully impressionistic, and though it has more emotional impact than most of his stories, it is hardly sentimental. What strikes the reader is not just emotion, but the aptness of emotion. In this case the subject is the immature and wholly fantasized love of a young Irish lad for the village schoolteacher and the pathetic consequences of that love. It is framed as a tale, told by a lonesome old woman to a faceless first-person narrator. In the course of their conversation, the narrator asks a conventional question about her family and uncovers a story. She had but one son, she tells him, and "It is in the asylum in Cork he is on me these twelve years." Crying out her "sorrows like the wild birds," she relates with no reticence the story of her son's infatuation for Miss Regan. "Denis was such a quiet boy, no way rough or accustomed to the girls at all—and how would he in this lonesome place?" The bleakness of the place is as congenital as the boy's desperate grasp for love.

The moment of crisis in the old woman's queer tale occurs when the boy's love erupts as violent madness. Haltered to his bed by neighbors and waiting for asylum officials, the boy calls for the schoolmistress. Astonishingly, she comes to the distressed cottage and in a totally selfless way sleeps next to the boy until dawn. Thus comforted and his "love" consummated, the boy leaves peacefully. The old woman, her eyes bright with profound emotion, recalls to the silent listener that the "strange and wonderful thing" is that "from that day to the day she left us there did no one speak a bad word about what she did, and the people couldn't do enough for her." The only possible way to follow that is to turn outward, which is precisely what O'Connor does in the final sentence. "Darkness had fallen over the Atlantic, blank grey to its farthest reaches." For O'Connor the story lies not in what the woman tells her visitor but in why she told it at all. Her tale is a resigned gesture that releases her for a moment from the restrictions of her isolated existence.

O'Connor's so-called "lyrical" stories leave little doubt about the power of his prose to evoke highly poetic visual images. One of the most intriguing of these is "Uprooted," a story about two brothers, a teacher and a priest, both frustrated by the present and cut off from the past. Ned Keating, the teacher, is bored in Dublin by routine and judicious patterns. Tom, the more spontaneous and vigorous of the two, is a curate in Wicklow. Together they visit their home in the west. O'Connor's descriptions and conversational exchanges are forthright and swift. The momentum of the story is fierce, disallowing deep speculation. Neither of the brothers has time to think, time to be nostalgic, or time to regret. They are bustled about, sharing hospitable drinks and meeting forgotten relations. On the island home of their mother's people they enjoy the company of young people. Ned enjoys a moment of physical attraction:

> Everything had darkened and grown lonely, and with his head in the blinding folds of the shawl which reeked of turf-smoke and his arm about Cait, Ned felt as if he had dropped out of Time's pocket.

Ned is caught between pensiveness and desire. In the boat back to the mainland "an extraordinary feeling of exultation and loss" descends upon him.

The end of the story is sullen; the next morning the brothers share in drowsy recollection their distraught night. Ned is troubled by Cait, of course, and the shadowy possibility of marriage. Tom's turmoil is more profound, suggesting a false vivacity the day before. Almost in confession the young priest despairingly asserts: "'You have something to look forward to. I have nothing. It's the loneliness of my job that kills you. Even to talk about it would be a relief, but there's no one you can talk to. People come to you with their troubles, but there's no one you can go to with your own.'" Tom is cut off by the demands of the cloth from the affections and

joys of life. O'Connor locates both men in the "sub-
junctive"—Tom for his vicarious experience of human
relationship and Ned for his reticence toward love. The
committed priest thinks of what might have been and the
uncommitted teacher of what might be, but rather than
go back on choices once made they simply fall back into
"Time's pocket." As the two brothers leave home, the
reader gets the distinct feeling that he is watching the
final uprooting of the two men in a moment of suspended
time. In the "magical light" of dawn over Cariganassa,
Ned's loss is the loss of childhood, of an intolerably
vivid world. His future is as "remote and intangible" as
Tom's is futile and lonely. The lyrical moment is the uprooting itself, the suspending of human personality
between the irremediable past and the intractable future,
between promise and regret.

The sensitive treatment of Tom Keating should not be
construed as strictly indicative of O'Connor's response
to the Church in Ireland. In many ways, O'Connor was
more fiercely anticlerical than most Irish writers, having
bolted from the Church during the Rebellion. Perhaps
realizing the need for detachment, he wrote scarcely at all
about the priesthood before *Crab Apple Jelly*. What is
remarkable about the seven stories in this volume is not
the number of priests, but the variety of ways O'Connor
looks at them. Priests as persons with human needs and
weaknesses concern him more than priests as institutional representatives. "Song Without Words" is a
simple tale about two monks, trapped in silence and
saintliness, who share a common weakness—gambling.
Human nature stands aligned against the scruples of
conscience. Far from being institutional iconoclasts, the
two monks are simply lonely persons, circumscribed

within arbitrarily impersonal limits. Gambling does nothing more than sweeten momentarily their silent prison. The old parish priest and his young curate in "The Star That Bids the Shepherd Fold" are as divided as the two monks are close. An encounter with a dignified and cosmopolitan captain of a French ship in Cork harbor accentuates that difference. The two priests board the ship to retrieve one of the girls of the parish. The curate, who speaks some French, at least attempts to communicate, but his superior maintains his authoritarian pose. The captain refuses to accept his impertinence and suggests that the girl is probably their mistress. When they retreat, the parish priest is defiant, while the curate, the narrator observes, could only feel "hopeless and lost."

Father Ring, a man bent on filling the coffers of the Church, appears in three stories. In "The Miser" he is seen systematically bilking a cranky old shopkeeper only to be frustrated in the end. Even after ripping up every board in the miser's house, Ring is unable to find the fortune. One would think he was a hard-driving businessman who had just lost a close bid on a lucrative contract rather than a priest who just lost a parishioner. In the other two stories, Father Ring is mentioned only in passing. He is feared and hated. None of the characters use the deferential "Father" when speaking of him: it's always just plain "Ring" and the tone is outright contempt.

However, to O'Connor the inhibiting effect of the church represented only a local manifestation of the deeper, more complex problems of individual people. Such stories as "The Luceys" and "The Mad Lomasneys" contain O'Connor's finest and most perceptive consideration of Ireland's Catholic middle class. He once said that "The Luceys" was a story he had struggled savagely with. As it appears in *Crab Apple Jelly* "The Luceys" is a highly dramatic story, relying heavily on dialogue and resembling, to an extent, a broadcast script, which it became. It is the story of the "constricted lives" people lead in small Irish towns, of the bitterness and misunderstanding that keep people apart.

The root occasion of "The Luceys" is the embezzlement of considerable money by Peter, Tom Lucey's son, and the divisive effect it has on the family. Ben, an accountant familiar with the financial back roads of the town, refuses to get involved. He says that he is afraid of reprisals from the men done out of their money. Yet it is respectability, that peculiar orthodoxy of Irish life, that motivates Ben's decision. Peter, of course, is banished and, predictably, killed in an accident. Tom refuses Ben's commiseration, accusing him of hating Peter all along, of being jealous of his son's advantages. Charlie, unspectacular but humane and sensitive, is trapped between his father and uncle.

Though the Luceys are worked upon by exterior forces —especially the venial climate of an Irish provincial town—they make their own tragedy. By keeping the issues contained, O'Connor has managed to magnify the people enough to give their "tragedy" significance. O'Connor himself insisted that "Tom Lucey is trapped in his own pride, Ben Lucey in his good-natured worldliness and Charlie in the intensity of his family feeling." The tragedy is in the failure to understand the situation —Ben fails to "arrange" the account books and Tom fails to break his word. Charlie, who first urged his father to use his influence in Peter's behalf and then pleaded

with his uncle to relent and visit Ben's deathbed, is one
of those men to whom easy certainty of absolute truth is
not available. Charlie stands, as I think O'Connor
seemed to stand, always between conflicting priorities,
isolated by integrity and sensitivity.

O'Connor once said that "An Irish writer without
contention is a freak of nature. All the literature that
matters to me was written by people who had to dodge
the censor." The sexual repression of middle-class Irish
life provided more than one Irish writer ready material
for fiction. Even as the "in" Irish writer was expected to
attack the clergy, so he was expected to "shock" Irish
readers with a little sex, or to expose ruthlessly the sexual
blight of a parochial society. O'Connor avoided both
subjects until *Crab Apple Jelly*, refusing to wage a token
war, to stoop to rhetoric. Later he was censored and to
some he is only remembered for that. "The Mad Lomasneys" is one of his earliest and one of his most successful
stories about the strange way of love among the Irish.
The relationship of Ned Lowry and Rita Lomasney
engages O'Connor's singular attention in the story from
their first, awkward encounter as adolescents to their
strained and unfortunate parting. Rita is an independent,
rather rash girl, with a manner best described as audacious and a voice that seems to laugh casually at life.
Ned is rather unperturbably automatic, though also
"clever . . . precise and tranquil." But O'Connor is not
just juxtaposing the predictable and the unpredictable.
He is carefully accenting the subtle games played by the
middle class. Consequently, much of the story takes the
same dramatic form as "The Luceys," so that despite a
lapse of time the effect is intensely immediate.

In the second section of the story Rita appears suddenly back home, having left her job as a teacher in a small rural community. With an impertinent flip of her hair she explains to her curious sisters about the unsatisfactory end of her first affair. "'There was only one man in the whole blooming village and he was a bank clerk. We called him "The One." I wasn't there a week when the nuns ticked me off for riding on the pillion of his bike.'" She explains that because his mother wanted him to be a priest any flirtation was taken grimly. Ned, a regular visitor to the Lomasney home, responds in a measured and unsurprised manner. "As he was understood to be in love with Rita, this wasn't quite what Nellie expected."

Rarely does O'Connor play the symbol game or manipulate a story with devices. However, in this story cigarettes serve to accentuate the self-consciously adult mannerisms of both Ned and Rita. Cigarettes emphasize Ned's calculated equilibrium; smoking gives him time to secure his position. Cigarettes underscore Rita's impulsive and rebellious nature. After pouring tea for Ned and whiskey for herself, Rita continues her curious assault on his sensibilities: "'You may think you're a great fellow, all because you read Tolstoy and don't go to Mass, but you'd be just as scared if a girl offered to go to bed with you.'" At the same time she gestures for a light. It's all part of the game they are playing. Later when he admits that he would marry her, she abuses him for not asking before she went off to teach. Once again the cigarette figures in; frustrated by her malicious flourish, Ned squelches "the butt of his cigarette on his plate" and offers to repeat his proposal of marriage every six months. The waiting game and the stalling game are played quietly and brutally in a tidy, virtuous, if smoky, middle-class parlor in Cork.

Rita's theatrical manipulation of people continues to complicate her life. Another suitor, Justin Sullivan, proposes to her with the same effect—distraction and frustration. Finally, the entire Lomasney family is drawn into her curious and impudent game.

> Kitty and Nellie began to squabble viciously with Justin. They were convinced that the whole scene had only been arranged by Rita to make them look ridiculous. Justin sat back and began to enjoy the sport. Then Ned Lowry struck a match and lit another cigarette, and something about the careful quiet way he did it drew everybody's attention. Rita came back, laughing.

The upshot of all this madness is that she marries Justin rather than Ned. Still, O'Connor has not taken us far enough, and though resolution is not generally appropriate to his stories, he nevertheless must end with an occasion more telling than this.

The final section contains no surprises, no sentimental revelations, no reversals, and no vindications. Rita marries and Ned begins to see "a gentle, humorous girl with a great mass of jet-black hair, a snub nose, and a long, pointed melancholy face." He continues to visit the Lomasney family but seldom sees Rita. When they do meet she is tart, but he takes her in "his usual way, without resentment." During one of her staged scenes, Rita pokes fun at Ned's Spanish-looking friend and asks, "'Would Senorita What's-her-name ever let you stand godfather to my footballer, Ned?'" Once again the cigarettes appear. Ned calmly forces the issue until Rita admits that she never really wanted to marry anyone after Tony, the bank clerk. "I made up my mind that I'd marry the first of you that called." Capricious and unreason-

able, perhaps a trifle mad, but it is a way of solving a dilemma forced upon her as much from without as from
within. She would never admit that she married the wrong
man. "She looked mockingly at Ned, but her look belied
her. He rose and flicked the ashes neatly into the fire. Then
he stood with his back to it, his hands behind his back,
his feet spread out on the hearth." Ned's façade collapses
momentarily. He hurls the last remnant of distance, of
equilibrium, into the fire, the demands of the love game
having finally taken their toll of him.

The stories of *Crab Apple Jelly* represent the refinement
of O'Connor's technique of exploiting the "tone of a
man's voice, speaking." He didn't see life steadily or
whole; he heard it in bits and snatches. He once said in a
radio broadcast that he knew to the last syllable how any
Irishman would say anything—not what he would say,
but how he would say it. He maintained intimacy by
listening carefully. Nowhere is his attention to voices
more evident than in "The Long Road to Ummera," a
simple tale about an old woman's eccentric wish to be
buried in the mountain home of her people. By his own
admission the main voices were those of his own father
and grandmother. The story begins: "Always in the
evenings you saw her shuffle up the road. . . ." The narrator is personal and informal, speaking about his own
neighbors, not about strangers. Thomas Flanagan takes
this fidelity to the community to be contradictory to
O'Connor's theory of the "lonely voice." But his lonely
figures are usually trapped within their community. The
old woman in "The Long Road to Ummera" who wishes
to be buried at Ummera, the mountain home of her
people, speaks entirely within the idiom of her adopted
community. To her son this request is out of fashion and

impractical. She persists in her madness, entices a neighbor to drive her into the mountains, and is thwarted only by her physical weakness. With little elaboration and less comment O'Connor ends his story: "They brought her the long road to Ummera, the way she had come from it forty years before." Her frustrated and conventional son utters her strangely appropriate epitaph: "'Neighbors, this is Abby, Batty Heig's daughter, that kept her promise to ye at the end of all.'" The voice is lonely though it speaks within the community; O'Connor's voice is lonely not in spite of his fidelity to the community but because of it.

By the time O'Connor left Ireland he had begun to concentrate on fiction of a more private focus. Before the appearance of "The Drunkard," "Christmas Morning," and "My Oedipus Complex" he used first-person narration sparingly, and then generally as an interlocutor retelling a story told to him. The involvement of the narrator in "The Long Road to Ummera" or "Peasants" is genuine but not personal. However, one of the best stories in *The Common Chord*, "Judus," is the hilarious account by a settled bachelor of his first courtship; whether it was also his last we can only guess. He chuckles at his naive fantasies and foolish antics. But he fails to comprehend what the reader can't miss—his tragic dependence on his mother. O'Connor had listened to Irish life with brutal honesty. What he found was that people make themselves miserable, that they delude themselves, that they act in silly, indiscreet, or even vicious ways in spite of everything they know to the contrary. When he turned to situations closer to himself, his honesty still prevailed. He resisted the temptations of misanthropy and self-indulgence by adhering strictly to the limitations of his aesthetic: he was an observer, not a judge or an exhibitionist.

Larry Delaney, the quixotic narrator of almost half of the stories in *Traveller's Samples* and *Domestic Relations,* talks casually about various ludicrous moments in his childhood and adolescence. In a sense Larry is recreating himself; he is at once puppet and puppeteer. He thoroughly enjoys the comic absurdities of his past, especially the disparity between what he knows now and what he knew back then. In "The Idealist" he proves himself to have been a liar, in "Christmas Morning" a thief. He also reveals his Oedipus complex, his first confession, and his first drunk. About the only thing he doesn't reveal is his first lay. He thinks of himself as wise and self-aware. What he saw in a more innocent day as mountains, he can now laughingly dismiss as molehills. The tone of these stories is gentle and forgiving, but the reader gradually must wonder about Larry's reliability. The child's irrationality may appear absurd in relation to adult rationality, but no more absurd than adult irrationality from a child's point of view. O'Connor's irony, as usual, is doubly refracted. The progression in the stories from a five-year-old boy in "My Oedipus Complex" to a young man in his early twenties in "Private Property" and "The Paragon" suggests something close to a cycle. However, there is little progression of either knowledge or freedom. One can make too much of Larry's role as a unifying figure; but then, one can make too little of it, too. O'Connor neither excuses Larry's ineffectiveness nor condemns his impulsive misadventures. Remarkably, the stories are almost completely devoid of nostalgia.

The first story of *Domestic Relations* is called "The

Genius." It begins like "The Idealist," with an eccentric quip by Delaney: "Some kids are sissies by nature but I was a sissy by conviction." Instead of joining the usual neighborhood games, he calculates that a genius should be an explorer. All of O'Connor's juveniles seem to have astonishing fantasy-producing faculties. Generally, this activity has a kind of smug, pretentious air to it. Not only does Larry appear disdainful of other kids, he is self-righteously superior to his parents. If he is not playing one off against the other, he is patronizing them. (Of his father he observes, "He had never expected to be the father of a genius and it filled him with forebodings.")

His endless and trivial questions upset his father and intrigue his mother. The main question in this story concerns the origin of babies. Patiently his mother manufactures a metaphor about engines in mummies and starting handles on daddies. Armed with this great knowledge, Larry goes off in search of girls. He makes a fool of himself by explaining all about babies to an older girl he has decided to love. Like anyone who talks too much, Larry regrets most of it. He is jilted for an older boy, of course, and his entire world crumbles. He finds little comfort in his mother's assurance that he would find new friends; people not involved in such great tragedy never appreciate its enormity. O'Connor ends on a note that gives the whole story substance: "For all the difference it made, I might as well become a priest. I felt it was a poor, sad, lonesome thing being nothing but a genius." O'Connor's kids are people above all else, and like most people they are lonely, misunderstood, and trapped by their own misconceptions.

"The Man of the World" finds Larry and an older boy resorting to binoculars in order to learn exactly about the mystery of sex. But there is more in the story than one boy learning from another how to masturbate or smoke. O'Connor carefully constructs a web of visual effects in the story to accent the central activity of snooping. For all their elaborate plans, the boys only witness the evening prayers of a young couple. Jimmy Leary, who appears to Larry nonchalant throughout the ordeal, is proud of the achievement. But Larry, who like all of O'Connor's juveniles suffers from guilt as well as fantasy, is embarrassed. He says:

> beyond us watching the young married couple from ambush, I had felt someone else watching us, so that at once we ceased to be the observers and became the observed. And the observed in such a humiliating position that nothing I could imagine our victims doing would have been so degrading.

Words such as "ambush" and "victims" pinpoint the sense of degradation. The reversal of observer and observed is a subtle way of dramatizing human finitude in contrast to a larger and unknown universe. The dark tone of the conclusion gives poignant testimony to O'Connor's serious purpose in these stories. Larry cannot pray, only speculate that he will never be as sophisticated as his friend, "never able to put on a knowing smile, because always beyond the world of appearance I would see only eternity watching." However, O'Connor refuses to leave the story hanging in meditative abstraction. He abruptly brings us back with this final remark by Jimmy: "'Sometimes, of course, it's better than that. ... You shouldn't judge it by tonight.'" Obviously Jimmy hasn't shared Larry's shattering experience. What "revelation," after all, isn't lonely? But O'Connor may have also introduced an element of doubt: will Larry take part in another ambush despite the guilt and good intentions of the moment?

The most enjoyable story in *Domestic Relations* is "Daydreams," in which Larry recreates an incident that happened to him when he was nineteen. Out of work and short of funds, he either walked the streets or read in the public library, always dreaming of women. While sauntering along a river bank one evening with no cigarettes and no tram fare, he hears a scream and is confronted by a woman sobbing over the loss of two nights' work to a "dirty rat." Larry immediately takes up the prostitute's cause with romantic ferocity. He retrieves her money and is rewarded by a couple of quid stuffed into his jacket.

The adventure in itself is entertaining, especially the generous irony of Larry's total lack of awareness. But idealists and reformers seldom lack self-righteousness. When it does dawn on Larry that he has just acted out one of his daydreams, his conscience is touched by having taken pay for acting as gallantly as he had always hoped he would. So at the foot of Summerhill he gives an old beggar woman the two pounds solely on impulse. Immediately the imprudence of that act strikes him: "I knew it was wrong, the exhibitionistic behavior of someone who was trying to reconcile the conflict in himself by a lying dramatic gesture. Next day I would be without cigarettes again and cursing myself for a fool. I was really destitute now, without money or self-respect." He submits to reality and finds a job, but by the time he saves enough to repay the girl she is gone, to Liverpool, he surmises, or "Glasgow or one of the other safety-valves by which we pious folk keep ourselves safe in our own daydreams." One has only to read *An Only Child* or *Irish Miles* to see that there's a lot of Frank O'Connor in that story.

The rest of the stories in *Domestic Relations* are about outcasts of every sort—ugly ducklings, orphans, pariahs, paragons—all persons who, like Sherwood Anderson's "grotesques," assume that their desires and fancies are abnormal. Displaced from home or family, these persons suffer from delusions of grandeur or degradation, simply because they don't communicate with people enough to discover that everyone else has the same needs and fears. "Private Property" and "A Bachelor's Story" both hinge on betrayal; in the first a young man is betrayed by revolution, in the second by romantic love. In both instances, an individual is victimized by his abstractions. "The Pariah" and "Expectation of Life" are about so-called "bad marriages." Though O'Connor indicates that the tragedy or disappointment of these people is their own fault, his tone is never arrogant or patronizing. In "Orphans," for instance, a faceless narrator tells a story about a woman who once lived across the road. His manner is casual and unassuming. His language has the same chatty, idiomatic ease of the stories Larry Delaney tells about himself. The woman had married the brother of her first lover. Why she married him, against all good judgment, is the gist of the story. The narrator concludes: "Like all earnest people, Hilda went through life looking for a cause, and now he was her cause, and she would serve him the best way she knew." The irrational behavior of people hardly amazes O'Connor at all. In fact, if people always acted according to rational standards, if they never acted impulsively or imprudently then there would probably be very little for him to write about. Prudence, then, may be next to prudishness on

O'Connor's list of repressive and dehumanizing forces.

Not long after the publication of *Domestic Relations*, O'Connor returned to Ireland, the only vital source of imaginative energy for him. There was certainly no instant infusion of energy into his writing. But there appeared a renewed vigor, even an occasional flash of petulance, that made his last work fresh, though slightly uneven. *A Set of Variations*, twenty-seven stories written mostly in the 1960s, is not his best collection but it does suggest that in the last few years of his life Frank O'Connor had returned to whatever it was that produced the stories of the 1930s. Throughout the volume he is turning old sod, sifting through old themes, returning to old loyalties. However, the book is hardly the work of a tired old man resurrecting past glories. Rather, it is the work of one whose hand is steady, whose eye is keen, and whose voice is clear. As a whole, *A Set of Variations* has a range of interest and style comparable to *Crab Apple Jelly*. The domestic relations are mainly adult relations. In fact, there are more stories about old people and about death than in any previous volume. But O'Connor could never be grim or morbid; his humor is as wry as ever.

In O'Connor's "juvenile" stories, from "The Drunkard" and "Christmas Morning" to these later stories, one of the prominent elements is the tension between parents. In fact, without such underlying emotional tension the devious plans of the children would be almost neutralized. Time and again in O'Connor's family situations what is generally construed as a valuable trait proves to be harmful—a mother's love smothers the child, or a father's understanding lenience is taken as indifference. In the same manner, what is generally taken as harmful or weak (irrationality, brutality, or indifference) can often produce unexpected good—a drunken child preserves his father's sobriety and a father's flippant responses to honest questions serve to cushion an eventual disillusionment.

One of the most subtle stories in *A Set of Variations* concerns precisely this emotional chaos. In "Out-and-Out Free Gift" a perfect blend of considerate parents and dutiful child is upset by the normal insubordinations of a sixteen-year-old. A detached narrator looks back to show just how perfect a family it was. Ned Callahan and his wife Celia were always understanding and sensitive. Jimmy was a perfect son who trusted their judgment. Ned, for instance, having an incurable sweet tooth, persuaded Jimmy during the war to barter his own sugar for toys. The lesson, he said, was that "There is no such thing in business as an out-and-out free gift." Later Ned worked hard to understand Jimmy's problems. He chose Jimmy's school and scrupulously arranged his son's life. "It is a wise father," the narrator observes, "who can persuade his son of anything of the sort." O'Connor's irony is humane but unmistakable.

With the disintegration of Jimmy's manners and honesty, Ned's persuasive control is shattered. His sensitive talk makes no more impression on his son than the eventual appeal to force. Forbidden to associate with a boy Ned considers a "waster," Jimmy defies the order and lies to check his father's indignation. Ned challenges his contention that he was at one house and not at the forbidden one. Upon checking Jimmy's story Ned finds, of course, that the people hadn't seen Jimmy for some time. The lady admonishes Ned not to "be too hard on him! Sure, we were wild ourselves once." Looking back at the woman waving to him from the lighted doorway,

Ned is "touched by this glimpse of an interior not so un-
like his own but seen from outside, in all its innocence."
The idea goes by without fanfare, but it is crucial to Ned's
final recognition. He turns from what appears to be a
perfectly harmonious family to his son, standing in the
roadway not in defiance but in weary despair. Viewed
from without, Jimmy's story is a challenge and Ned's
response is anger. But viewed from within, it becomes
frustration, and Ned can only sigh hopelessly. All the
superficial games of family unity are just window-dress-
ing put up to cover a messy interior. Jimmy had chosen
the Ryan house because it provided an image of the
domestic tranquillity he wanted. His fantasy had fractured Ned's false picture of himself and his relationship
with Jimmy. All Ned would ever know "was that somewhere behind it all were despair and loneliness and terror,
under the magic of an autumn night."

However, an O'Connor story seldom ends so easily.
The potential tragedy vanishes with the morning. Where
Ned is cold and aloof, "more from embarrassment than
hostility," Jimmy is helpful and warm. He even punc-
tures Ned's considered balloon with a jibe about sugar.
That evening Celia observes that Jimmy has actually
improved. Ned, too honest to take credit, just shakes his
head and confesses that he has done nothing at all. Then
in that soft irony wives reserve for their husbands, Celia
assures him that he must have said something, after all,
"There's no such thing in business as an out-and-out
free gift." Among other things, O'Conner has suggested
that kids probably raise themselves, that talk usually fails
to affect genuine communication, and that in the end
most problems are solved by circumstance rather than
choice.

A "bad marriage" is a battlefield without diplomacy.

In most social division there is, in fact, division; the
contenders can separate to allow wounds to heal and
emotions to unwind. But in marriage the individual's
identity is always exposed, always on the alert. Generally,
the cause of dissension in marriage is principle, some
abstraction taken by one partner or the other to be a
source of individual strength. "A man's loneliness is his
strength," O'Connor writes in "The Cheat," "and only
a wife can really destroy him because only she can understand his loneliness." For Dick Gordon, the young Cork
engineer in that story, religious tolerance is the besetting
strength. By marrying a Protestant girl he broadcasts his
carefully cultivated "reasonableness," that proud loneliness of the man above sectarianism. As the title implies,
the crisis of the story is infidelity, but not, as one might
expect of a writer of banned books, sexual infidelity. By
accident Dick Gordon learns that his wife has been re-
ceiving instruction from a priest. Dick's facade of control
collapses; his wife has made a fool of him. The narrator's
comment is simply that she has fooled herself, "persuaded herself that he was dull and tolerant and gentle
and that nothing she did would affect their relationship.
It is the weak spot in the cheat, man and woman."
There is the guts of the story. Dick Gordon's identity is
wrapped up in fighting the easy way. Barbara plays the
cheat by depriving him of the object of his tolerance.

Marital problems generally cause widening ripples of
public involvement. The narrator casually remarks that
"it was old Ned Murphy who said the thing that stuck."
With two of Dick's friends drinking one night, Murphy
sourly says, "'It's like your wife having an affair with
another man.'" In this tidy scene O'Connor's knack
for milking the slightest gesture of every drop of insight

is evident. The two friends, Cashman and Enright, laugh louder than the bachelor Murphy. The analogy is uncomfortably apt to them; "both were married men and there had been a scandal about Enright's wife, who had had an affair with a commercial traveler." The narrator adds that they both always knew there was "another man" in the background, "a shadowy presence, not as real as they were." Cashman contends that he must have given her cause, as if there's a cause for every human failing. Murphy pontificates that religious girls like that shouldn't marry optimists like Dick Gordon, because "optimism is the plague of a religious mind. Dick has no notion of how intolerable life can be. A man like that doesn't even believe in evil."

Though certainly not one of his best stories, "The Cheat" nevertheless reveals O'Connor's return in his last years to the emotional gravity of his early fiction. Curiously he has moved closer to himself while assuming once again a detached narrative voice. Dick Gordon is more or less a dramatization of O'Connor himself, of his own persistence and petulance. Dick Gordon dies with only a vague kind of solace.

O'Connor opens "The School for Wives," another story about a bad marriage, with the generalization that "the real trouble with love is that people want contradictory things out of it." In this story a young rake marries a virtuous girl after a notorious career of "skirt-hunting." Giving up his old ways, he settles down to a successful law practice. His wife, however, wants the adventure he has tired of. When she seeks out his old crowd, a perfectly suitable marriage is fractured. Against his wishes she associates freely with his old friends, while he, growing more alienated all the time, becomes excessively religious. In "The American Wife," neither the wife nor her Irish husband are able to get beyond the silly abstraction of nationality. O'Connor knew that such abstractions as religion and nationality are true to the extent people hold them to be. Elsie is the chattering American who glorifies Irishmen; with a wink O'Connor adds that this "did not go down too well in Cork, where men stood in perpetual contemplation of the dangers of marriage." Tom, the man she marries, is unable to break away from Cork, though he knew he "belonged to a country whose youth was always escaping from it, out beyond the harbor, and that was middle-aged in all its attitudes and institutions." Elsie shuttles back and forth to America, giving birth to babies conceived in Cork. Only Tom's friend recognizes the "irremediable." Tom lives alone with pictures of his family; he may visit them in America, "but it is here he will return and here, no doubt, he will die." What is "irremediable" is probably one's attachment to home, no matter how dirty or venial it is, no matter how provincial or pig-headed its customs are. O'Connor is not above knocking holes in his own irrationalities, as "The American Wife" and "The Cheat" so nicely show. And that, I think, is what gives *A Set of Variations* its vigor, that quality of emotional vulnerability and personal venture.

One other story about the public spectacle as well as the private agony of a "bad marriage" deserves mention. In "The Impossible Marriage" a young man and woman, both burdened with possessive and selfish mothers, decide to marry but live separately. The marriage became "a matter of scandalous jokes, and remained so as long as it lasted." "This marriage that seemed to end at the church door was a mockery" of all that the pious neighbors believed in, "so they took their revenge as people will whose dearest beliefs have been slighted." Eileen and Jim have a patchwork marriage, but they are happy. From the outside it is only an imitation of marriage, but examined from within it is more real than most. After the death of Jim's mother, Eileen's mother refuses to move. Two years later Jim dies and Eileen insists that she'll never marry again: "People can't be as happy as that a second time, you know." The neighbors come to believe that "in spite of everything she had been intensely happy, happy in some way they could not understand, and that what had seemed to them a mockery of marriage had indeed been one so complete and satisfying that beside it, even by their standards, a woman might think everything else in the world a mere shadow." The tragedy is also a shadow, a reflection of those who see from the outside only. From within, the story is as warm and affirmative, as emotionally vulnerable, as "Michael's Wife."

Perhaps the most intriguing stories in *A Set of Variations* are those at the end of the volume about priests. Father Ring, the ubiquitous confidence man of *Crab Apple Jelly* and *The Common Chord*, has vanished. In his place are some completely human priests more along the line of the hard-nosed old priest in "The Sentry" or the frustrated curate in "Uprooted." Most of these stories concern Father Fogarty, a lonely man bearing strong resemblance to O'Connor's friend Father Tim Traynor. Moreover, all of the Fogarty stories deal with death. Stunned by the death of a seminary friend, Fogarty in "The Wreath" travels to the funeral only to get in an argument with the parish priest over a wreath that has turned up on the coffin. To the older man such a thing is "against the rubrics" and is bad custom besides. Fogarty insolently comments, "'You mean Masses bring in more money.'" The priest's rationale is that "flowers are a pagan survival." Fogarty rages for part of the story about the stupidity of the parish priest and muses the rest of the time about who could possibly have sent a wreath. After some discussion with the relatives of the dead priest, Fogarty and his blunt friend Father Jackson convince them that to take away the wreath would be to "throw mud on a dead man's grave." Standing with the other priests at the grave, Fogarty glances from their grim faces to the wreath.

> Each time it came over him in a flood of emotion that what he and Jackson had saved was something more than a sentimental token. It was the thing which formerly had linked them to Devine and which now linked them with one another; the feeling of their own integrity as men beside their integrity as priests; the thing which gave significance and beauty to their sacrifice.

"The Teacher's Mass" reveals even more about Fogarty's profound sense of humanity. A bit of the devil was always roused in him by Considine, the old schoolmaster who served as acolyte for the curate's Mass. The description of Considine, who "had all the childish vanity of the man of dissociated scholarship," and who "wrote occasional scurrilous letters to the local paper to correct some error in etymology," suggests that O'Connor may have been at least as anti-academic as anticlerical. Fogarty, on the other hand, leans toward "action and energy. . . . He was an energetic and emotional man . . . Women were less of a temptation to him than the thought of an active instinctual life." Despite a lingering illness, Considine persists in his habit of serving at the early Mass, until one morning he dies in the middle of the Mass on the altar steps. The effect on Fogarty is sharp:

> When he turned to face the body of the church and said *"Dominus vobiscum,"* he saw as if for the first time the prostrate form with its fallen jaw and weary eyes, under the light that came in from the sea through the trees in their first leaf, and murmured *"Et cum spiritu tuo"* for the man whose spirit had flown.

Recognizing something apart from obstinacy in the old man's passion, Fogarty has simply allowed him to die in harness. The old man, after all, represented something that made him conscious of his own human weaknesses.

The final story of the volume is "The Mass Island" with Father Fogarty figured in death. Romantic to the end, Fogarty has requested that he be buried on an island in one of the lakes in the south of Ireland. To Father Jackson the notion is "sheer sentimentality." He recalls the time Fogarty had lured him there. Jackson then was put off by the very thing Fogarty loved about the place and its people—"the overintimacy of it all." He proceeds with the arrangement anyway, because, as he notes wearily, romantics always leave their "worldly friends to carry out their romantic intentions." As it turns out, hundreds of villagers in mid-winter show up at the island for the burial. Jackson realizes that he and the staid parish priest "would never earn more from the people of the mountains than respect; what they gave to the fat, unclerical young man who had served them with pints in the bar and egged them on to tell their old stories and bullied and ragged and even fought them was something

infinitely greater." On the causeway the cars have some
difficulty until one driver turns his headlights directly on
the island.

> One by one, the ranked headlights blazed up, and at every
> moment the scene before them grew more vivid—the gate-
> way and the stile, and beyond the causeway that ran toward
> the little brown stone oratory with its mock Romanesque
> doorway. As the lights strengthened and steadied, the whole
> island became like a vast piece of theatre scenery cut out
> against the gloomy wall of the mountain with the tiny white-
> washed cottages at its base.

The moment is a triumphant moment for Fogarty and
for the instinctive way of life. O'Connor has not only
beatified a friend, he has spoken eloquently for his own
outlook.

The title story, "A Set of Variations on a Borrowed
Theme," is an even finer and more serene affirmation of
the imaginative way of life. It is about an old woman, one
of that most neglected group of people who are believed
to have outlived their usefulness. Instead of retreating
gracefully into her daughter's care after her husband's
death, Kate Mahoney decides to take in a foster child to
preserve her home, her independence, her vitality. Obstinate in the face of her daughters' selfish notions of family
image and her neighbors' petty concern over respectability, Kate eventually takes in two illegitimate boys. The
piety of those about her and the argument of her tired,
rheumatic body notwithstanding, she persists simply
because "Motherhood was the only trade Kate knew."
Somehow she manages to make a secure home for herself
and the boys. Though the narrator calls her a "dreamer"
and though she knows herself to be something of an old

fool, she is not senile nor is her search for dignity cast as odd by O'Connor. To him the needs of old people, like the needs of kids perhaps, are no less human and real than the needs of men and women raising families, administering businesses, and managing the world's affairs. Likewise, the self-delusions and perversities of youth and age are no more excusable than those of "responsible" men and women.

More than likely, then, O'Connor has borrowed a theme from himself. Indeed the story is a kind of compendium of O'Connor notions. First off, Kate and the boys are outcasts, lonely people forced to live at the fringe of society and to adopt radically creative measures to cope with existence. Kate is reminiscent of any number of O'Connor's dreamers. The boys are illegitimate, recalling a reviewer's complaint that his stories seem too full of bastards. Kate's daughters and her neighbors are the respectable middle-class Irish Catholics who usually make O'Connor's hair stand on end. There are at least two wayward girls and one drunken father. Then, predictably, the story is set in Cork. The boys, like Larry and Sonny in "Christmas Morning," represent two sides of O'Connor's own personality. Jimmy, the "pirate chief," angrily insists on undertaking a search for his father. James, the "quiet scholar," is content to make his mark in the world before uncovering his past. Yet both indulge the backward look and both are aware of a dubious paternity. They are also aware of motherhood, in a biological and in a spiritual sense. Kate, a sixty-year-old version of Mary Kate McCormick, is as persistent and as intuitive as O'Connor's own mother seems to have been.

Yet with all these "variations" the story is far from

cluttered. Uncharacteristic of an O'Connor story, it covers a rather extended period of time. But it is sparse and direct, with an almost perfect balance between narration and dialogue. Finally, as with so many of his stories, O'Connor ends with a disturbing wrinkle. Kate is dying and there is a sense of finality. Everything to this point fits; the reader has even begun to feel that assurance of resolution. All four of her "children" are standing near the deathbed. Taking the boys' hands, she tells them how proud she is. After a moment's thought she adds "something that shocked them all. 'And yeer father is proud of ye, I'm sure.'" One of the daughters corrects her saying urgently, "'Mammy, 'tisn't who you think. 'Tis Jimmy and James.'" Kate's reply, with open eyes, is cold and straight: "'Excuse me, child, I know perfectly well who I have.'" Later the daughters and the neighbors who come to say a final prayer ask the same question: "How could a woman who was already old take the things the world had thrown away and out of them fashion a new family, dearer to her than the old and finer than any she had known?" Kate's old crony Hanna Dinan has the last word: "'Wisha, wasn't she a great little woman! She had them all against her and she bested them. They had everything, and she had nothing, and she bested them all in the end!'" What is real, in the end, is not the normal, the logical, or the predictable, but the imaginative improvisation.

4

Conclusion: A Backward Glance

Scanning the entire course of Frank O'Connor's literary career, one is above all impressed by a remarkable unity of purpose working through a maze of conflicting impulses. He was a person of fierce sympathies. His idealism was often too buoyant, his bitterness often too heavy. But when it came to his writing he was a model of discipline and control. What this indicates, I think, is that though he lost his innocence at Gormanstown, he never really ceased to be a romantic, by which he meant a way of seeing things, a style of life at once impulsive and searching. He rejected the romantic aesthetic, which he saw as the sentimental indulgence of the trite emotion, the reliance on the nostalgic or rhetorical generality. Likewise, he rejected the realistic way of seeing things— the "sensible" compromise, the cynical indifference to human needs, or the sterile, academic appraisal of life. But he completely affirmed the realistic aesthetic—the careful manner and sensitive frankness that are the trademarks of his writing from first to last.

Unquestionably, O'Connor's early writing represents some of his very finest work. His early stories and essays are especially impressive for the exuberance of their concerns and the unpretentious clarity of their style. His first volume, *Guests of the Nation*, was mainly about the insurrection. The energy of the entire volume emanates equally from O'Connor's unrestrained youthfulness and his idealistic fervor. That he later repudiated this early mode of writing does not repudiate its idealism. The violence of "Guests of the Nation" is a fresh, even creative sort of thing; but for him to have indulged it would have been to stagnate. Though he moved away from violence, he nevertheless continued for some time to operate within a context of youthful vigor. For example, his two novels, written while he was still trying to decide whether or not to write at all, were boldly uncertain efforts. In the first, *The Saint and Mary Kate* (1932), O'Connor's sympathetic idealism was too buoyant to control. In the second, *Dutch Interior* (1940), the unnaturally obtuse form was too flimsy to support the weight of O'Connor's embittered social criticism. Like the poems he was writing at about the same time, the novels were improvisational and imbalanced. But where the poems exhibited a mannered facetiousness, the novels were extremely serious and personal.

One of O'Connor's pet critical assumptions was that a person's art is an allegory of his life; one writes what he is. To that extent, then, his own writing is autobiographical. His two novels, especially, revealed his vacillation between such "counter-truths" as realism and romanticism, objectivity and subjectivity, judgment and instinct. After *Crab Apple Jelly* (1944), after the war and the dissolution of his personal life, his stories, too, became more personal. The voice was no longer that of the detached and irascible observer of the early stories, but of a man speaking for himself about his childhood. At the same time, acutely conscious of the danger of easy subjectivity and unbridled emotion, O'Connor concentrated almost exclusively on form and design. Perhaps, feeling too close to the issues and the characters, he simply pressed for detachment by way of technique. Emotion and lyrical expressiveness seem to have been suspended while O'Connor foraged about for something genuine in a more or less transitional society. Ireland in the 1940s and early fifties was trying to decide whether or not to enter the twentieth century. O'Connor was caught between a painful past and a dubious future. So he simply gave up one lost cause—saving Ireland from itself—and turned with equal intensity and honesty to another— himself.

All in all, the story of Frank O'Connor is the story. Invariably, his imagination forced itself through the picturesque, the historical and the abstract to some story, some point of vivid impact. For him human dignity and rationality inevitably yield to the sudden impulse, to the unpredictable and passing moment. O'Connor believed that it is "not for nothing that some of the great story-tellers . . . have been tramps." O'Connor himself was not a tramp like Maxim Gorki, nor was he a stage Irishman like Brendan Behan. But he was nothing if not displaced, so perhaps he is one who "stands always somewhere on the outskirts of society, less interested in its famous and typical figures, than in the lonely and gnarled and obscure individuals." After all, culture to the story-teller is a highly fragile thing, united not by generalities but by the inconveniently diverse lives of common folks. To O'Connor a story, whether it was about the Nun of Beare, Michael Collins, the Rock of Cashel, or those "displaced persons" of Cork, was nothing less than a "lyric cry in the face of destiny."

Frank O'Connor's stories were a sort of personal revolution. He took the form seriously and stayed with it despite modest financial benefits and pressures for a "major work." Only a secure vision of man and of himself as an artist explains this dedication to the Irish "common reader" and his constant focus on the "little guy." Everything he wrote displays his improvising and contending spirit, but his stories speak most eloquently of his lonely struggle for integrity and freedom. If any single attitude consistently looms large in O'Connor's work, it is a distrust of human reason, a suspicion of the abstract or the unnatural. Yet ironically, the principal strategy of his stories is containment, a deliberate scaling down of issues, situations and techniques. Simplicity requires conscious discipline and superb control —it's hard to be easy. A "lonely, personal art" is a hidden kind of thing. Consequently, O'Connor's stories appear so effortless and perfect that some readers, as Benedict Kiely noticed, have assumed that "he is all surface and no depth." Actually, Kiely cautions, O'Connor "touches depth . . . without any of the creaking machinery or obvious attempts to be significant that make so much modern literature ludicrous." O'Connor revised his stories constantly, cutting away the extraneous, the nostalgic, the doctrinaire, the trite. When the story was free—free from self-conscious art and superficial thought —Frank O'Connor, at least for a moment, was free. He once said that where Yeats, Synge, and the rest have their "presences" to offer eternity, "I have only my voices." When all is said, his stories will stand as his most enduring contribution to modern literature and to Irish life.

Selected Bibliography

Primary Material

SHORT STORY COLLECTIONS

Guests of the Nation. London: Macmillan, 1931; New York: Macmillan, 1931.

Bones of Contention. London: Macmillan, 1936; New York: Macmillan, 1936.

Crab Apple Jelly. London: Macmillan, 1944; New York: Knopf, 1944.

The Common Chord. London: Macmillan, 1947; New York: Knopf, 1948.

Traveller's Samples. London: Macmillan, 1951; New York: Knopf, 1951.

The Stories of Frank O'Connor. New York: Knopf, 1952; London: Hamish Hamilton, 1953.

Domestic Relations. New York: Knopf, 1957; London: Hamish Hamilton, 1957.

A Set of Variations. New York: Knopf, 1969. *Collection Three.* London: Macmillan, 1969.

TRANSLATIONS FROM THE IRISH

The Wild Bird's Nest. Dublin: Cuala Press, 1932. A limited edition, with an introductory essay by Æ.

Lords and Commons. Dublin: Cuala Press, 1938. A limited edition.

The Fountain of Magic. London: Macmillan, 1939.

Lament for Art O'Leary. Dublin: Cuala Press, 1940. A limited edition, with illustrations by Jack B. Yeats.

The Midnight Court. A Rhythmical Bacchanalia from the Irish of Bryan Merriman. Dublin: Fridberg, 1946.

Kings, Lords, & Commons. New York: Knopf, 1959; London: Macmillan, 1961.

The Little Monasteries. Dublin: Dolmen, 1963. A limited edition.

A Golden Treasury of Irish Poetry, edited with David Greene. London: Macmillan, 1967.

LITERARY CRITICISM AND HISTORY

Towards an Appreciation of Literature. Dublin: Metropolitan, 1945.

The Art of the Theatre. Dublin: Fridberg, 1947.

The Road to Stratford. London: Methuen, 1948. Revised as *Shakespeare's Progress*. Cleveland: World, 1960.

The Mirror in the Roadway. New York: Knopf, 1956; London: Hamish Hamilton, 1957.

The Lonely Voice. Cleveland: World, 1962; London: Macmillan, 1963.

The Backward Look: A Survey of Irish Literature. London: Macmillan, 1967. American Edition, *A Short History of Irish Literature: A Backward Look*. New York: Putnam, 1967.

NOVELS

The Saint and Mary Kate. London: Macmillan, 1932, 1936; New York: Macmillan, 1932.

Dutch Interior. London: Macmillan, 1940; New York: Knopf, 1940.

AUTOBIOGRAPHY

An Only Child. New York: Knopf, 1961; London: Macmillan, 1962.
My Father's Son. London: Macmillan, 1968; New York: Knopf, 1969.

TRAVEL (IRISH INTERESTS)

Irish Miles. London: Macmillan, 1947.
Lenister, Munster, and Connaught. London: Robert Hale, 1950.

BIOGRAPHY

The Big Fellow: A Life of Michael Collins. London: Nelson, 1937. American edition, *Death in Dublin: Michael Collins and the Irish Revolution*. New York: Doubleday, Doran, 1937.

POETRY

Three Old Brothers. London: Nelson, 1936.

MAJOR ESSAYS

"Two Friends—Yeats and Æ," *Yale Review* (September, 1939).
"To any would-be writer," *The Bell* (March, 1941).
"The Future of Irish Literature," *Horizon* (February, 1942).
"James Joyce—a Postmortem," *The Bell* (February, 1942).
"Ireland," *Holiday* (December, 1949).
"And It's a Lonely, Personal Art," *New York Times Book Review* (April 12, 1953).
"A Lyric Voice in the Irish Theatre," *New York Times Book Review* (May 31, 1953).

"Adventures in Translation," *Listener* (January 25, 1962).
"Censorship," *The Dubliner* (March, 1962).

Secondary Material

Breit, Harvey. "Frank O'Connor," in *The Writer Observed* (Cleveland, 1956).

Brenner, Gerry. *A Study of Frank O'Connor's Short Stories.* Dissertation, University of Washington, 1965.

Kavanagh, Patrick. "Coloured Balloons—a study of Frank O'Connor," *The Bell* (December, 1947).

Kavanagh, Peter. *The Story of the Abbey Theatre* (New York, 1950).

Kiely, Benedict. *Modern Irish Fiction: A Critique* (Dublin, 1950).

Mercier, Vivian. "The Irish Short Story and the Oral Tradition," in *The Celtic Cross: Studies in Irish Culture and Literature,* ed. R. B. Browne, et al. (Purdue, 1964).

Saul, George B. "A Consideration of Frank O'Connor's Short Stories," *Colby Library Quarterly* (December, 1963).

Sealy, Douglas. "The Translations of Frank O'Connor," *The Dubliner* (Summer, 1963).

Share, Bernard. "O'Connor's Unflattering Picture of Bourgeois Ireland," *Hibernia* (January, 1965).

Sheehy, Maurice, ed. *Michael/Frank: Studies on Frank O'Connor* (New York, 1969). Includes essays by Richard Ellmann, Roger McHugh, Brendan Kennelly, David Greene Thomas Flanagan, and others.

Taylor, Geoffrey. "The Poetry of Frank O'Connor," *The Bell* (December, 1945).